MY DAY! MY DREAM! MY DESTINY!

Date:

To:

From:

Message:

You Can Do More Than Survive, You Can Succeed!

TOTAL RECALL
ACE EVERY TEST EVERY TIME

Food Is for the Body
Education Is for the Mind
Poetry Is for the Soul

Sharon Esther Lampert

#1 Poetry Website for Student Projects
www.WorldFamousPoems.com
The Greatest Poems Ever Written
on Extraordinary World Events

The Restless Sunrise

A Streaming Golden Light
Enters In and Under the Windowsill

A Restless Sleeper
Is Awakened to New Beginnings

To Catch a Sunrise
The Dreamer Arises as the Light Bursts Forth

The Sunrise Lights Up the Sky
In Anticipation of a World

That Has Yet To Be Created.

Sharon Esther Lampert

Also By The Author

Student Empowerment Tools
for Academic Success

- EVERY DAY AN EASY A
- TOTAL RECALL: ACE EVERY TEST EVERY TIME
- Your Study Room Is Under New Management
- Smartgrades School Notebooks with Study Skills
- WRITERS RUN THE WORLD: College English Bootcamp!
- LEARN ENGLISH

Parent Empowerment Tools
for Academic Success

- How to Parent for Academic Success
- Broken Wings Blocked Blessings

Teacher Empowerment Tools
for Academic Success

- The Silent Crisis Destroying America's Brightest Minds ("Book of the Month" Alma Public Library, Wisconsin)
- The Universal Gold Standard of Education
- How Does Learning Take Place

Psychological Empowerment Tools
for Academic Success

- Integration Therapy: 14 Steps to True and Everlasting Happiness
- How to Stop Paying for the Sins of Your Parents
- Lost, Bad, and Evil: The Root of All Evil Is Child Abuse

Children's Book
The Smartest Children's Book In The Whole World
Learn New Vocabulary with Color-Coded Words
SCHMALTZY: IN AMERICA EVEN A CAT CAN HAVE A DREAM
The Cat Who Helps Children Learn, Love, and Laugh
THE WORLD FAMOUS PIANO VIRTUOSO
BOOKWORM CHILDREN'S BOOK AWARD
schmaltzy.com

TOTAL RECALL
ACE EVERY TEST EVERY TIME

SHARON ROSE SUGAR

SMARTGRADES
BRAIN POWER REVOLUTION
www.smartgrades.com

SMARTGRADES College Edition

TOTAL RECALL: ACE EVERY TEST EVERY TIME

©2024 ©2012 by Sharon Rose Sugar. All Rights Reserved. No part of this book may be used or reproduced in any manner whatsoever without written permission, except in the case of brief quotations embodied in critical articles and reviews.

College Edition
ISBN Hardcover: 978-1-885872-51-7
ISBN Paperback: 978-1-885872-44-9
ISBN E-Book: 978-1-885872-20-3

Library of Congress Catalog Card Number: 2009903306
UPC: 672180

SMARTGRADES
BRAIN POWER REVOLUTION

Smartgrades.com
EverydayanEasyA.com
PhotonSuperhero.com
BooksnotBombs.com
Schmaltzy.com
SharonEstherLampert.com
WorldFamousPoems.com

SMARTGRADES books may be purchased for education, business, or sales promotional use.

To Order Books:
Ingram, Phone: 615-793-5000
Baker and Taylor, Phone: 800-775-1800

Book Interior and Cover Design By Sharon Esther Lampert
Illustrations: By Mark A. Hicks, illustrator. Used with permission.
For more information, please visit websites:
www.MARKIX.net and www.markix.net/4teachers.html

First Edition

Manufactured in the United States of America

8 Goalposts of Education

1. Education: Knowledge!
2. Enlightenment: AHA!
3. Empowerment: Yes I Can!
4. Excellence: Mastery!
5. Emancipation: All Can Do!
6. Egalitarianism: Equal Rights!
7. Equality: New World Order!
8. Economic Stability: World Peace!

Sharon Rose Sugar
The Paladin of Education for the 21st Century

SMARTGRADES
INSTANT AND TOTAL RECALL
ACE EVERY TEST EVERY TIME

Sharon Rose Sugar
Paladin of Education

What All Parents Need to Know About Their Child's Education
THIS BOOK SAVES LIVES
"The Silent Crisis Destroying America's Brightest Minds"
"Book of the Month" Alma Public Library, Wisconsin

RETENTION, RECOGNITION, RECALL

TOTAL RECALL: ACE EVERY TEST EVERY TIME

SMARTGRADES
SUCCESS STRATEGY STUDY SKILLS

Our books include the **SMARTGRADES** Learning Skills and Life Skills that will empower you for personal success at home, academic success in school, and professional success in the workplace.

SMARTGRADES Time Management Skills:
- **SMARTGRADES** Homework Action Planner
- Setting Priorities Tool
- Divide and Conquer Tool
- Estimate and Actual Time Log Tool
- Detours, Delays, and Distractions Tool

SMARTGRADES In-Class Skills:
- Prereading Tool
- Active Listening Tool
- Note Taking Tool
- Abbreviation Tool
- Questioning Tool
- Test Preview Question Tool

SMARTGRADES At-Home Skills:
- Organization Tool
- **SMARTGRADES** School Notebooks
- Study Room Tool
- Study Strategy Tool
- Subject Strategy Tool
- Power Study Snack Tool
- Manage Anxiety, Stress, and Depression Tool

SMARTGRADES Reading Skills:
- Speed Reading Tool
- Reading Comprehension Tool

SMARTGRADES Test Preparation Skills:
- Processing Tools for Instant & Total Recall to Ace Tests

SMARTGRADES BRAIN POWER REVOLUTION

SMARTGRADES Writing Skills:
- Outlining Tool
- Annotating Tool
- Summarizing Tool
- Paraphrasing Tool
- English Essay Tool
- Research Paper Tool
- Citation Tool
- Proofreading to Perfection Tool

SMARTGRADES Thinking Skills:
- Critical Thinking Tools
- Creative Thinking Tools
- Scientific Thinking Tools
- Mathematical Thinking Tools

SMARTGRADES On-Test Skills:
- Multiple Choice Tool
- Essay Exam Tool
- True False Tool
- Matching Tool
- Fill In the Blank Tool
- Identity Exam Tool
- Verbal Analogy Tool
- Oral Exam Tool
- Open Book Tool
- Take Home Tool
- Standardized Exam Tool

SMARTGRADES Career Skills:
- Career and Personality Tool
- Summer Internship & Life Experience Tool
- Networking Tool
- Entrepreneur Tool
- Job Tool
- Career Tool

© 2000. All Rights Reserved. SMARTGRADES INC., smartgrades.com

TOTAL RECALL: ACE EVERY TEST EVERY TIME

Sugar's 7 Grade A Facts of Academic Success

Fact 1. Your Brain Is a Powerful Biological Machine
Put your hands on your head and feel your brain. Your brain is the most powerful biological machine in the world. This book is your instruction manual. It will show you how to maximize your brain power. Facts are food for the brain. You will spend most of your day eating facts and building your brain muscles. First, you will receive facts from your teacher. Second, you will process the facts using the **SMARTGRADES SUCCESS STRATEGY**. Third, you will return the facts to the teacher in a essay, research paper, or on a test.

Fact 2. Eat Right for the Energy to Learn
Before you can feed your brain the facts, you have to feed your body for the energy to learn. Healthy meals consist of carbohydrates, protein, fresh fruits and vegetables containing vitamins and minerals. To maximize your energy to learn, you will need sufficient sleep, good eating habits, and regular exercise. Junk food won't cut it. Avoid eating foods loaded with addictive sugar and salt and processed with chemicals that are devoid of nutritious vitamins and minerals.

Fact 3. The First Week of School
It only takes the first week of school for students to fall behind and start playing catch-up. You have to learn how to manage your time, and make every hour count.

Fact 4. School Is All About the Facts, Not About You
Your job is to **RETRIEVE** the facts from the class notes, handouts, and textbook, and then **RETURN** the facts to the teacher in an essay, research paper, and on a test.

Fact 5. 80/20 Rule
If you can send back 80% of the facts for a B grade, then you can send back the remaining 20% of the facts for an A grade.

Fact 6. What Are the Critical Hours of the School Day?
- Class Time: 1 Hour (fixed)
- Test Time: 1 Hour (fixed)
- Study Periods: (variable)

Fact 7. Every Day of the Week Is Test Preparation Day
Priority 1. Energy to Learn
Did you sleep well, eat right, and exercise for the energy to learn?

Priority 2. Manage Your Time
Do you have a **SMARTGRADES** Homework Planner to help you manage your time and multiple schedules?

Priority 3. SMARTGRADES STUDY SKILLS
Do you have **SMARTGRADES** School Notebooks that contain **SUCCESS STRATEGY STUDY SKILLS**?

Priority 4. Test Review Notes
Right after class, write **Test Review Notes** using the **10 STEP SMARTGRADES STUDY SKILLS** for Instant & Total Recall to ace your tests?

10 STEP SMARTGRADES SUCCESS STRATEGY
Step 1. Estimation
Step 2. Divide and Conquer
Step 3. Active Reading
Step 4. Extraction
Step 5. Condensation
Step 6. Association
Step 7. Test Review Notes
Step 8. Conversion
Step 9. Visualization
Step 10. Self-Test

SUPERHIGHWAY OF ACADEMIC SUCCESS

1. School Is All About the Facts

2. The Facts Are Always on the Move

In Class
Facts Move from a Blackboard into a Notebook

At Home
Facts Move into a Test Review Note,
Homework Assignment, Essay, and Research Paper

On Test
Facts Move Through Your Brain for Instant
and Total Recall and onto a Test

Education Is Measured By Three Criteria:
In-Depth Comprehension
Long Term Retention
Mastery of the Material

Sharon Rose Sugar
Paladin of Education

What All Parents Need to Know About Their Child's Education
THIS BOOK SAVES LIVES
"The Silent Crisis Destroying America's Brightest Minds"
"Book of the Month" Alma Public Library, Wisconsin

Attention All Earthlings!

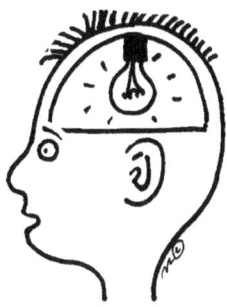

Put Your Hands on Your Head.
Your Brain Is the Most Powerful
Biological Machine in the World.
Your Brain Is Your Most Valuable Asset.
This Book Is the Instruction Manual for Your Brain.

Facts Are Food for Your Brain.
School Is a Restaurant and Facts Are on the Menu.
Eat the Facts and Build Your Brain Muscle.
Knowledge Is Power!
Good Grades Deserve Great Rewards!
Earn A Grade, Earn FREE Gift.

Make the Grade and Achieve Your Dream.
Every Student Is a Success Story!
Every Student Is Somebody Special!
MY DAY! MY DREAM! MY DESTINY!
LIVE YOUR DREAMS!

If You Need My Help, I Am at Your Service,

www.PhotonSuperhero.com

**MY DAY!
MY DREAM!
MY DESTINY!**

Contents

Chapter 1
Every Day Is Test Preparation Day
23

Chapter 2
Organize: Take Control of the Facts
33

Chapter 3
Eat Right and Sleep Well for Energy to Test
53

Chapter 4
Manage Your Test Anxiety
65

Chapter 5
SMARTGRADES SUCCESS STRATEGY
INSTANT AND TOTAL RECALL
75

Chapter 6
How to Ace Every Test Every Time
91

Chapter 7
Ace Your Test: English, History, Art, Science, Math
101

Chapter 8
Good Grades Deserve Great Rewards
159

Failing to Prepare Is Preparing to Fail

Chapter 1
Every Day Is Test Preparation Day

Mile by Mile, Life's a Trial
Yard by Yard, It's Not So Hard
Inch by Inch, It's a Cinch

Chapter 1

Every Day Is Test Preparation Day

Tools of the Trade

Manage Your Time

Steps to Success

Step 1. Write a "Daily Action Plan"
On a daily basis, you will have to learn how to manage your time to be able to read your textbooks, write your papers, and prepare to ace your tests.

Step 2. Manage Your Multiple Schedules
Your life will revolve around fixed and variable schedules, and you will need to write them down, analyze them, and reconfigure them, so that there is a seamless flow between them, instead of conflict, confusion, and chaos.

Schedule 1. Eat Right for Energy to Learn (variable)
Schedule 2. Class Schedule (fixed)
Schedule 3. Study Schedule (variable)
Schedule 4. Test Schedule (fixed)
Schedule 5. Exercise Schedule (variable)
Schedule 6. Part-Time Job Schedule (fixed)
Schedule 7. Family Chores Schedule (variable)
Schedule 8. Social Life Schedule (variable)
Schedule 9. Extra-Curricular School Activities (variable)
Schedule 10. Free Time (variable and negligible)

Plan Your Work and Work Your Plan

Don't Wish For It, Work For It

Success Comes in Cans, Not Cants

Well Done Is Better Than Well Said

The Only Something You Get for Nothing Is Failure

When You Lose, Don't Lose the Lesson

SMARTGRADES BRAIN POWER REVOLUTION

27

Write a Daily Action Plan

Eat Right for the Energy to Learn:
Fiber Breakfast: Power Lunch: Lite Dinner:

Daily Budget: $
Expense 1. $ Expense 2. $ Expense 3. $
Total Daily Expenses: $

Classes:
Subject: Time: Room:
Subject: Time: Room:

Study Period 1: (45 minutes each with 15 minute breaks)
Time: Study Area:
Eat a Study Snack to stay energized, e.g., apple, orange, grapes
- Read the class notes, handouts, and textbook ☐
- Write Test Review Notes (**SMARTGRADES STUDY SKILLS**) ☐

Daily Exercise Routine: Stretch, Walk, Bike, Jog, Sports

Study Period 2: (45 minutes each with 15 minute breaks)
- Seek approval from teacher for outline of paper ☐
- Preread next chapter of textbook ☐

Read a Daily Funny for Stress-Relief: HA, HA, HA, HA, HA, HA

Part-Time Job:

Family Chores:

Social Life:

Regular Bedtime: 10 p.m.   Actual Bedtime:

Daily Reward for a Job Well Done:

Q. What was the best part of day?

Q. What was the worst part of day: delays, detours, and distractions?

My Multiple Schedules Worksheet

Schedule 1. Eat Right for the Energy to Learn (variable)
M: Whole grains, protein, fresh fruits and vegetables
T:
W:
T:
F:
S:
S:

Schedule 2. Class Schedule (fixed)

M:

T:

W:

T:

F:

Schedule 3. Study Periods (variable)
M: Right after class, write your Test Review Notes
T:
W:
T:
F:
S:
S:

Schedule 4. Test Schedule (fixed)

Schedule 5. Exercise (variable)
M: Take a walk, jog around the track, or go for swim
T:
W:
T:
S:
S:

Schedule 6. Part Time Job (fixed)
M:
T:
W:
T:
F:
S:
S:

Schedule 7. Family Responsibilities (variable)
M:
T:
W:
T:
F:
S:
S:

Schedule 8. Extra-Curricular Activities (fixed)
M:
T:
T:
F:
S:
S:

Schedule 9. Social Life Schedule (variable)
M: School night
T: School night
W: School night
T: School night
F: Social Life
S: Social Life
S:

Schedule 10. Free Time Schedule (variable and negligible)

Take Control of Your Social Life Schedule

Keeping in touch with friends takes time. Pick a time to chat with your friends. Don't answer the phone and interrupt your study period every time a friend calls to talk with you, unless that friend is your study buddy. Pick a time after your school work is completed to make your social calls and stay connected to your loved ones.

Examples:

1. Suzy called about making a plan for Friday night

Action Plan: Call her back at 9:30 p.m.

Time Log

Estimated Time: 10 Minutes

Actual Time: 1 1/2 Hours

Error: 1 Hour and 20 Minutes

Speedbumps: Delays, Detours, and Distractions

Action Plan:

2. Peter called to have dinner on Saturday, date night

Action Plan: Call him back at 7:45 p.m.

Time Log

Estimated Time:

Actual Time:

Error:

Speedbumps: Delays, Detours, and Distractions:

Action Plan:

My Social Life Schedule (Variable)

Making new friends and keeping in touch with old friends takes time. Your friends will change over time and place.

Q. How often do you introduce yourself to a new person?
   a. Daily   b. Weekly   c. Monthly   d. Yearly

Here's how to introduce yourself to a new person:
1. Smile and make eye contact.
2. Say "Hello."
3. Ask a simple question? "What time do you have?"
4. Offer a compliment: "I love your blue sweater."
5. Introduce yourself: "My name is . . ."
6. What's your name?
7. Find common ground: _____
a. New study buddy
b. New girlfriend or boyfriend
c. New teammate for sports
d. New business partner for start-up internet business

Great relationships are based on connection, chemistry, compatibility, caring, communication, companionship, and common ground. When you meet someone, take notes:
Q1. What kind of connection do we have?
Q2. Do we have chemistry?
Q3. Are we compatible?
Q4. Is there genuine affection between us?
Q5. Do we have common interests?
Q6. Do we have honest communication?

A Place for Everything
Everything in Its Place

Benjamin Franklin

Chapter 2
Organize: Take Control of the Facts

Don't Agonize, Organize!
Florynce R. Kennedy

Chapter 2

Take Control of the Facts
Organize the Mountain of Academic Materials

Take control of the facts. School is a game of facts. Your job is to **RETRIEVE** the facts and **RETURN** the facts. First, you will retrieve the facts from the blackboard (class notes), handouts, and textbook, and then you will return the facts to the teacher in an essay, research paper, and on a test. You need to have an organization system in place to manage the voluminous academic facts.

For Example

Class: English

The academic facts come from 3 sources:
1. Class Notes
2. Handouts
3. Textbook

For each set of facts, you will write Test Review Notes. You will now have 3 sets of Test Review Notes:
1. Class Notes + Test Review Notes
2. Handouts + Test Review Notes
3. Textbook + Test Review Notes
4. Homework Assignments, Quizzes, and Tests

All of These Academic Materials Need to Be Organized

TOTAL RECALL: ACE EVERY TEST EVERY TIME

| Test Review Notes for Class notes | Test Review Notes for Textbook |

Blue Folder 1/English

| Class Handouts | Test Review Notes for Handouts |

Blue Folder 2/English

| Homework Assignments | Quizzes and Tests |

Blue Folder 3/English

Option 1. School Notebooks and Color-Coded Folders

Buy a school notebook for each class and buy color-coded folders to keep track of the following:
1. Test Review Notes (class notes, handouts, and textbook)
2. Quizzes
3. Tests
4. Homework Assignments

Buy Color-Coded Folders for Each Class:
English   Blue Folder
Math   Green Folder
Science   Yellow Folder
History   Purple Folder
Language   Red Folder

Label Your Blue Folders (3 Folders Per Class)
Folder 1. Test Review Notes
Pocket 1. Class Notes Test Review Notes
Pocket 2. Textbook Test Review Notes

Folder 2. Class Handouts
Pocket 1. Handouts
Pocket 2. Test Review Notes for Handouts

Folder 3. Homework, Quizzes, and Tests
Pocket 1. Homework Assignments
Pocket 2. Quizzes and Tests

BEFORE YOUR NEXT TEST INVEST IN THE ACADEMIC BEST

SMARTGRADES
School Notebooks
Good Grades Become Grand Dreams
www.smartgrades.com

5 ESSENTIAL STUDY SKILLS

Class Notes and Test-Review Notes in One Notebook

- How to Ace Every Test Every Time
- How to Ace a Multiple Choice Test
- How to Ace an Essay Test
- How to Write a Research Paper
- Homework Action Planner

BEFORE YOUR NEXT TEST INVEST IN THE ACADEMIC BEST

SMARTGRADES BRAIN POWER REVOLUTION

Option 2. SMARTGRADES SCHOOL NOTEBOOKS
You can take class notes and write **Test Review Notes** in the same notebook, **SMARTGRADES SUCCESS STRATEGY STUDY SKILLS** are at your fingertips. There is also a notebook for textbook **Test Review Notes** and research papers.

Academic Planner
Use a **SMARTGRADES** Planner to manage your schedules.

Notebook 1. Class Notes and Test Review Notes
Use a **SMARTGRADES** School Notebook for Class Notes and Test Review Notes.

Notebook 2. Textbook Test Review Notes
Use a **SMARTGRADES** School Notebook for Textbook Test Review Notes.

Notebook 3. Research Papers
Use a **SMARTGRADES** School Notebook to research a paper.

Handouts and Test-Review Notes
One color-coded folder for handouts and Test Review Notes

Homework, Quizzes, and Tests
One color-coded folder for homework, quizzes, and tests

The Smartgrades Advantage
- Buy a **SMARTGRADES** School Notebook and keep the receipt.

- 1000 Study Skills at Your Fingertips

- Earn A Grade, Earn Free Gift
  (mail in receipt as proof-of-purchase)

- **PHOTON SUPERHERO** will call you to congratulate you on your academic success!

TOTAL RECALL: ACE EVERY TEST EVERY TIME

How to Organize Your Study Area

Tools of the Trade

How to Choose a Great Study Area
How to Choose a Power Study Snack
How to Buy, Rent, or Borrow Textbooks
How to Choose a School Library Locker

Steps to Success

Right after class, you will immediately go to your favorite study area and write your **Test Review Notes**. You will read your class notes, handout, and textbook and use your **10 Step SMARTGRADES SUCCESS STRATEGY** for **Instant & Total Recall** to ace your tests (Chapter 7).

How to Choose a Great Study Area

- ❏ 1. Choose a study area with no external distractions
- ❏ 2. Spacious desk for notebook, textbook, and reference materials
- ❏ 3. Comfortable chair that fits your body type
- ❏ 4. Good lighting
- ❏ 5. Computer with internet connection, printer, ink, and paper
- ❏ 6. External hard drive for daily backups of school work

How to Choose a Power Study Snack

Learning requires a great deal of energy. Every two hours, you will need some nutrition. When you are hungry, you will start searching for food. You will waste a lot of time walking up and down the aisles of a supermarket, and will be tempted as a result of persuasive advertisements to choose some processed food in a plastic wrapper that is loaded with sugar and salt and is devoid of vitamins and minerals. Or you will succumb to eating greasy junk food that will leave you undernourished and fat.

On one hand, you may need that walk to stretch your legs and get some fresh air. On the other hand, there are too many temptations, and you will waste too much time and spend more money than your budget allows.

Make a Daily Power Study Snack Plan:

M: Yogurt, granola, and fruit
T: Bran muffin in a variety of flavors
W: Turkey sandwich with red peppers and cheese
T: Carrots and celery sticks with humus/peanut butter
F: TRAIL MIX of almonds, walnuts, cranberries, raisins

- Always carry a bottle of water with you to stay hydrated
- Avoid soft drinks loaded with sugar that make you fat

TOTAL RECALL: ACE EVERY TEST EVERY TIME

How to Buy, Rent, or Borrow Textbooks

❏ **Plan A.** Pay Full Price for Brand New Textbooks
Buy brand new textbooks at full price and later sell them to a used bookstore or to another student.

❏ **Plan B.** Pay Half Price for Used Textbooks
Buy textbooks at half-price by buying used textbooks. Checkout: Biblio.com, Abebooks.com, A1books.com, Maketextbooksaffordable.org, and Bookfinder.com.

❏ **Plan C.** Free Textbooks at the Library
Free copies of textbooks are in the school library.

❏ **Plan D.** Free Textbooks from My Friends
Students have used textbooks that they may give away for free because they are not in good shape.

❏ **Plan E.** Cheap Textbooks from My Friends
Students have used textbooks in good condition that they will be happy to sell for half price.

❏ **Plan F.** Share Textbooks with Your Study Buddy
If you are taking the same class with a good friend and study partner, buy one set of textbooks and share them.

How to Choose a School Library Locker

Lugging heavy textbooks is bad for your back and posture.

Q. Are you starting to slouch?

Most schools have lockers in the library. This is a great place for a locker because you can leave your heavy textbooks in your locker and study in the library. You won't have to carry heavy books back and forth from the library. You will also be able to place your supplementary library books into your locker.

First Come, First Serve
The top lockers are reserved early and first. If you wait too long to buy a library locker, you will have to buy a bottom locker that is adjacent to your knees.

To Do List: The School Library Locker
- ☐ 1. Call school library and ask if there are library lockers.
- ☐ 2. Go to the library and examine the lockers.
- ☐ 3. Pick a locker on the same floor as your major
     e.g., Major in Psychology, 4th Floor = Psych Books
- ☐ 4. Add your Smartgrades School Notebooks and text books to your locker. You can also add your gym clothes.
- ☐ 5. Checkout supplementary PSYCH textbooks that will help you learn the academic materials, and add to locker.

TOTAL RECALL: ACE EVERY TEST EVERY TIME

How to Preread a Textbook Chapter

Before class, preread the textbook chapter to increase your understanding and absorption of the academic material.

Step 1. Read the End-of-Chapter Summary
Read the end-of-chapter summary for an overview of the main points of the chapter.

Step 2. Read the Boldface Headings of the Chapter
Read for a general overview of the material of the chapter. Read the boldface headings and subheadings. Read actively with a pencil/highlighter in hand and write down the main idea and major and minor points of the chapter.

Main Idea:

Major Points:
1.
2.
3.

Minor Points:
1.
2.
3.

After Class Read Textbook for In-Depth Comprehension
After class, you will go back to your class notes, handouts, and textbook and read for in-depth comprehension and write Test Review Notes. You will use the **SMARTGRADES SUCCESS STRATEGY** to process academic material for **Instant & Total Recall** to ace your exams (CH 7).

Your Teacher's Office Hours

Here are nine very good reasons to visit your teacher:

☑ Visit 1: Introduction
Visit your teacher to introduce yourself.

☑ Visit 2: Seek Clarification
Visit your teacher to ask a question.

☑ Visit 3: Approval of Topic and Outline of Paper
Visit your teacher for approval of topic and outline of your paper.

☑ Visit 4: Approval of Rough Draft of Paper
Visit your teacher for approval of rough draft of your paper.

☑ Visit 5: Teacher's Comments
Visit your teacher to discuss comments on your paper.

☑ Visit 6: Unfair Test Question
Visit your teacher to complain about an unfair test question.

☑ Visit 7: Grading Error
Visit your teacher to complain about a grading error.

☑ Visit 8: Express Gratitude
Visit your teacher to say thank you to express your appreciation for a great class.

☑ Visit 9: Recommendation for Your Resume
Visit your teacher to ask for a recommendation to accompany your resume.

How to Develop a Study Group

Study groups can keep you and your friends on track for academic success. These groups help everyone because they facilitate the learning process by thinking out loud, sharing ideas, and learning from each other.

There are many benefits to forming a study group:
1. Improves your understanding of the material
2. Share your talents
3. Provides an emotional support system to motivate you
4. Learning can be drudgery and sharing the tedious task lessens the pain

Tools of the Trade

Q1. How many students?
Q2. Who should be in the study group?
Q3. Where should you hold the study sessions?
Q4. How long should a study session be?
Q5. When should the study group meet?
Q6. Who is the leader of the group?
Q7. What are the objectives and goals?

Steps to Success

Step 1. How Many Students?
The best size for a study group is four to six people. Small groups don't have man power to get things done. Large groups are harder to manage.

Step 2. Who Are the Members?
The best study groups are composed of individuals who share the same interest in doing well in class and on tests. Everyone has different strengths and weakness. By participating in a study group you are able to benefit from the talents of other group members.

Step 3. Where Do We Meet?
Study group sessions should be held in a location where you can talk and bring your power study snacks. The best place is an empty classroom, office space or dining room table.

Step 4. How Long Do We Study?
Study group sessions should be not longer than two to three hours. If the study session is too short, you can't accomplish anything. If it is too long, you loose interest and focus. Its best to schedule breaks every 45 minutes for a ten minute study snack.

Step 5. When Do We Meet?
Try to meet at the same time and place each week. Creating a set routine will help each member to plan ahead and come prepare to each session.

Step 6. Who Is the Leader of the Group?
Each group study session should have a leader. It's the leaders responsibility to make sure that the group is focused and stays on track.

Step 7. What Are the Objectives of the Study Group?
Doing well in school is all about retrieving the facts from your class notes, handouts and textbook reading assignments, and then returning the facts on a test. The facts have to be processed (absorbed) for **Instant & Total Recall** to ace your tests.

TOTAL RECALL: ACE EVERY TEST EVERY TIME

Each member can contribute their own particular strength to the group. Instead of one student doing all of the study tasks, they can be divided up among the study group. It is best to make a list of the tasks and divide and conquer, as follows:

Example: Divide Up Academic Tasks Among Members

1. One member takes copious notes in class.

2. One member collates the best supplementary reading materials to further a deeper understanding of the material.

3. One member has a good reparte with the teacher, visits the office once a week, and has a crystal clear understanding of the teacher's expectations.

4. One member collates old exams for practice test questions.

5. One member prepares power study snacks.

6. Three members divide up writing Test Review Notes
    a. Class Notes Test Review Notes
    b. Handouts Test Review Notes
    c. Textbook Test Review Notes

7. One member prereads the chapter, takes notes, and hands them out an hour before class.

What Is Your Learning Style

How to Understand Your Learning Style

Identifying and understanding your learning style is critical to your study preparation. By knowing how you learn best you can select a school, class, teacher, textbook, and ultimately a career that appeals to your unique way of learning things.

Tools of the Trade

Visual (most common)
Auditory (languages, music)
Tactile (kinesthetic)
Logical (mathematical)
Social (interpersonal)

Steps to Success

Read definitions below to figure out how you learn best.

Visual Learning Style
Students learn best when ideas or subjects are presented in a visual format, with pictures, diagrams, videos or overhead projectors.

Auditory Learning Style

Students are able to learn, understand and retain information better when they hear it rather than see it. Students learn by participating in class discussion, by listening to a teacher lecture, or listening to audio tapes. For example, students who excel at learning languages and composing music are auditory learners.

Tactile Learning Style

Tactile learners are hands-on learners. They learn by touching and feeling. They learn best when they are able to physically participate directly in what they are required to learn or understand. For example, students who excel at work which requires hands-on skills, such as dentistry, surgery or carpentry.

Solitary Learning Style

Students who are private, introspective and independent. They are able to concentrate and focus on a specific project without outside help. Solitary learners prefer to work on problems in isolation. For example, writers, scientists, and entrepreneurs are solitary learners.

Logical Learning Style

Students who prefer to use their brain for logical and mathematical reasoning prefer the logical learning style. Logical learners can recognize patterns easily and are good at making logical connections between what would appear to most people to be meaningless content.

Social Learning Style

Students who communicate well will others, both verbally and non-verbally. Social learners prefer learning in groups or classes and typically like to spend one-on-one time with a teacher or an instructor. For example, teachers and therapists are good listeners and are able to understand other's views.

Q1. What is your learning style?

Q2. How does understanding your learning style help you to make informed choices about your destiny?

Q3. Do you now understand why you would rather go to your room and write a book or become a teacher and work with a group, rather than work with your hands and become a dentist, like your father?

Q4. What career choices fit your learning style best?

Energy Is Eternal Delight

William Blake

Chapter 3
Eat Right and Sleep Well for the Energy to Test

TOTAL RECALL: ACE EVERY TEST EVERY TIME

Q. Are You Hungry for the Energy to Learn?
Big Breakfast: Oatmeal, Banana, Cinnamon
Power Lunch: Big Plate
Light Dinner: Small Plate
Study Snacks: Apple, Carrot and Celery Sticks

Chapter 3

Eat Right for the Energy to Test

Q1. What Did You Eat this Morning?
You can't learn on an empty stomach. It takes energy to learn. Energy comes from good nutrition and sufficient sleep. First you feed your body with food, and then you feed your mind with facts.

Your electrical appliances will not work without a boost of electricity, and your brain will not work without a boost of whole grain fiber, protein, fresh fruits and vegetables loaded with natural (not synthetic) vitamins and minerals.

Think of yourself as a car with a gas tank that has to be filled up to be able to take you places. First, you fill your tank and then you drive. First, you eat a nutritious meal and then you go to school to learn. If you don't eat properly, your brain will not have the "FULL GAS TANK" to be able to read, think, question, research, write, memorize, and test.

Q2. Did You Put Some Love Into It?
Learning requires love. You have to put love into everything that you do. Your heart and your mind have to be working together as a team. According to the poet, philosopher, and educator, Sharon Esther Lampert, "You don't find love, you create love." Love has to be created. Like a warm and cozy fire on a cold winter's night, you have to create love for it to exist in the world.

TOTAL RECALL: ACE EVERY TEST EVERY TIME

Q3. Did You Laugh Today?

Learning requires a sense of humor. The learning curve is steep. It takes time to learn. Learning requires trial'n'error. Learning requires patience and practice until mastery is achieved. Sometimes you will have to get it all wrong, before you can get it all right. It is best to not take yourself so seriously, and to learn to laugh at yourself from time to time as you will often stumble blindly in the dark trying to figure out what your strengths and weaknesses are, where you belong in the world, and how you can make a difference and, ultimately, a contribution of meaningful significance.

Try not to let a day go by without a laugh that will bring a smile to your face. Late night TV talk shows use the daily newspaper as a spring board for spinning human trials and tribulations into comedy. The day may start out bleakly, but it always ends with a laugh. But don't stay up late to watch these TV shows, rather watch the reruns on the internet the next day, and go to bed at a decent hour. Almost every TV show is recorded on the internet, so you can watch them at your convenience, when you need a study break and a good laugh.

The Best Study Break Is the Website T.E.D.

T.E.D. is a website showcasing interesting people in the world, who make a difference. These people are hardly ever featured on TV. These people will inspire you, as you embark on your own academic journey in search of a purpose in life that is imbued with passion and prosperity.

Change Your Knowledge Base

Quite often, you will have to change your "Knowledge Base." To move forward in the world, you will have to leave the past behind, and get on a new road that will take you to a new place that is entirely different from where you came from and what you were taught.

Old Knowledge Base: "I can eat anything I want, as long as I eat in moderation."

New Knowledge Base: "I can't eat anything I want because the processed food is loaded with salt, sugar, corn syrup, and a whole host of chemicals and preservatives that I can't pronounce, spell, or remember.

Here are a few of the consequences of eating processed food:
- My body will not have sufficient vitamins and minerals

- I will always feel tired and want to eat more junk

- My body will overeat processed food trying to get energy from the food

- I will become overweight and undernourished

New Knowledge Base: Avoid Processed Food

I will not eat anything wrapped in plastic that can live for more than ten years in my knapsack, including those packaged protein bars (loaded with sugar).

TOTAL RECALL: ACE EVERY TEST EVERY TIME

How to Eat Right for the Energy to Test

You are a biological machine that needs fiber fuel to be able to think, read, research, write, memorize, and test. Before you leave for school, you need to have a system in place to manage your energy needs.

Fiber Facts
Whole Foods = Long-Term Energy

My 30-Second Breakfast
- Grab a bran muffin (try a different flavor each day)
- Grab two hard-boiled eggs (protein)
- Grab fruit: banana, apple, and orange (vitamins)
- Grab a container of orange juice (hydration)

My One-Minute Breakfast
- A slice of whole grain toast, cheese, tomato (fiber)
- Grab two hard-boiled eggs (protein)
- Grab fruit: banana, apple, and orange (vitamins)
- Grab a container of orange juice (hydration)

My Five-Minute Breakfast (Breakfast of Champions)
- A bowl of delicious and creamy oatmeal, add walnuts, sliced banana, cinnamon, and maple syrup. Drink a glass of orange juice.

My Power Lunch (Big Plate)

Fill big plate with 1/4 fist-sized protein and 3/4 vegetables
Monday: Fish with spinach, carrots, grilled red peppers
Tuesday: Meat with broccoli, carrots, corn
Wednesday: Fish with spinach, carrots, cauliflower
Thursday: Meat with green beans, carrots, corn
Friday: Fish with spinach, carrots, grilled red pepper

My Lite Dinner (Small Plate)

Fill small plate with 1/4 fist-sized protein and 3/4 vegetables
1. Eat off of a small plate to reduce your portion size
2. Eat dinner before 7 p.m.
3. Fill up on salad, vegetable soup, steamed vegetables
4. Avoid fried, fatty, and greasy food
5. Avoid heavy foods that put you to sleep after a meal
6. Avoid foods with sugar that keep you up late at night
7. No caffeinated drinks after 5 p.m. (poor sleep)

My Power Study Snacks for the Energy to Learn

1. Golden delicious apples with peanut butter or cheese
2. Fresh berries with yogurt and nuts, add honey
3. Carrot and celery sticks with humus
4. Bran muffins (cranberry, banana, carrot, apple)

TOTAL RECALL: ACE EVERY TEST EVERY TIME

Make Your Own Food Plan for Energy to Test

My 30-Second Breakfast

Whole Foods (long-lasting energy):

_____

Protein: _____

Vegetables: _____

Fruits: _____

Hydration (sugar free): _____

My One-Minute Breakfast

Whole Foods (long-lasting energy):

_____

Protein: _____

Vegetables: _____

Fruits: _____

Hydration (sugar free): _____

My Five-Minute Breakfast

Whole Foods (long-lasting energy):

_____

Protein: _____

Vegetables: _____

Fruits: _____

Hydration (sugar free): _____

SMARTGRADES BRAIN POWER REVOLUTION

My Power Lunch (Big Plate)

Protein: Fish/Meat/Beans _____

Vegetables: _____

Fruits: _____

Hydration (sugar free): _____

Low Fat Dessert: _____

My Light Dinner (Small Plate for Small Portions)

Protein: Fish/Meat/Bean _____

Vegetables: _____

Fruits: _____

Hydration (sugar free): _____

Low Fat Dessert: _____

No Caffeine After 5 p.m. (poor sleep, tired next day)

My Nutritious Study Snacks for the Energy to Learn

Monday: _____

Tuesday: _____

Wednesday: _____

Thursday: _____

Friday: _____

Saturday: _____

Sunday: _____

TOTAL RECALL: ACE EVERY TEST EVERY TIME

Get a Good Night's Sleep for the Energy to Learn

Tools of the Trade
Establish Your Bedtime Rules

Step to Success

Step 1. Establish a Bedtime Routine
Maintain a regular bedtime. You should go to bed, and wake up, at the same time each day. This will help your body to get into a sleep rhythm and make it easier to fall asleep and get up in the morning.

Example
- Regular bedtime on school nights is 10-11 p.m.
- Regular bedtime on the night before a test is 10 p.m.
- Friday and Saturday night bedtime is 12-1 a.m.
- Sunday night bedtime is 10:30 p.m.

Step 2. Sleep in a Dark Room
Sleep in complete darkness. The tiniest bit of light in the room can disrupt your circadian rhythm and your pineal gland's production of melatonin and seratonin.

Step 3. After 5 p.m., Don't Consume Caffeine

Avoid caffeine in coffee, tea, or soda after dinner. Caffeine does not always metabolize efficiently and therefore you may feel the effects long after consuming it (poor sleep, tired the next day)

Step 4. TV Is a Stimulant that Effects Your Sleep

No TV right before bed. It is too stimulating to the brain and it will take longer for you to fall asleep (poor sleep, tired the next day).

Step 5. Bathroom Bedtime Ritual

Go to the bathroom right before bed. This will reduce the chances that you'll wake up to go in the middle of the night.

Step 6. Avoid Drinking Before Bedtime

Don't drink any fluids within 2 hours of going to bed. This will reduce the likelihood of needing to get up and go to the bathroom.

Step 7. Use Your Bed Just for Sleeping

Keep your bed for sleeping. If you are used to watching TV or doing work in bed, you may find it harder to relax and to think of the bed as a place to sleep.

SMART POWER IS BACK IN THE HANDS OF ALL STUDENTS

PHOTON'S
Spiritual Illuminations 8 Superpowers of Stress-Relief

1. RECOGNIZE Your Star Qualities.

2. LISTEN to Your Inner Voice.

3. PROTECT Your Needs and Desires.

4. Have COURAGE to Abandon Relationships with insensitive people.

5. Attach Your HEART to Your HEAD and Make Decisions in Your Best Interest.

6. EMPOWER Yourself to Make the Necessary Changes to Ensure Your Happiness.

7. Have the VISION to See Beyond Present Difficulties and Create a Stress-Free Lifestyle.

8. Take Good Care of Yourself, You Belong to You.

PHOTON
SUPERHERO OF EDUCATION
www.BooksnotBombs.com

WORLD PEACE IS COMING TO PLANET EARTH

Chapter 4
Manage Your Test Anxiety

If You Learn Anything at Cornell,
Please Learn to Ask for Help.
It is a Sign of Wisdom and Strength

David Skorton
President of Cornell University

(2010: Six Student Suicides in Six Months)

According to the Jed Foundation,
it is roughly estimated that 24,000 suicide
attempts and 1,100 suicides occur annually among
U.S. college students aged 18 to 24 years
(The Jed Foundation, 2008).

Chapter 4

Manage Your Worry, Anxiety, Stress, and Bouts of Depression

Here are some of the reasons that most, if not all, students are anxious, stressed, and suffer "bouts of depression."

1. **Poor Time Management Tools:** Time cannot be saved. Students do not know how to take control of their time to make every hour count toward reaching their academic goals.

2. **Disorganization:** The academic facts are voluminous (class notes, handouts, and textbook) and students do not have an organization system in place to manage the mountain of facts.

3. **Energy Is Scattered in Too Many Directions:** Students are over scheduled. KEEP LIFE SIMPLE. Stick to your priorities of class, study period, part-time job, and exercise. Limit yourself to one or two activities a week, e.g., sporting event, music concert, or film.

4. **No Energy to Learn:** Students eat fast food, junk food and processed food devoid of nutrition.

5. **Poor Processing Tools:** Students wait until the night before a test to start memorizing academic material. Students do not have learning tools to process the facts for long-term retention to ace their tests.

6. **Financial Stress:** Students have not yet found their passion and purpose in life. Students are graduating with astronomical school loan debt and an insecure future.

7. **No Entrepreneurial Tools to Start Their Own Businesses:** Students are not required to take business classes, but 80% of all businesses are small businesses.

8. **Relationship Stress:** Students are trying to form an intimate attachment with a member of the opposite (or same) sex to form a partnership of mutual affection and admiration. Bonding your soul with the soul of another person for love, sex, and companionship is a challenging undertaking because both of you are still maturing and don't have defined identities. As a result, relationships are fragile. All breakups are painful to one degree or another.

9. **Worry, Anxiety, and Stress Can Escalate into Depression and Suicide:** Students feel overwhelmed by the demands of school, work, part-time jobs, and relationships (family, friends, and intimate partner). When disappointments build up, so does the emotional pain. The emotional pain can be too much to bear and depression will take hold of your soul and immobilize you.

LIFE IS UNFAIR
Everything Under the Sun Has an Expiration Date

Disappointments Multiply –>
Emotional Pain Is Too Much To Bear –>
Pain –> Rage –> Depression –>Suicide

For Example: This Student Is Having a Bad Week

1. Unfair Tricky Test Questions –> Emotional Pain
A student is sabotaged by unfair tricky test questions from a teacher with an ax to grind. You paid your tuition, studied for hours, and the entire class fails the test and it is graded on a curve. This teacher is undermining your self-confidence, destroying your self-esteem, and your dream for the future. Tip: Get the inside scoop on the class, before you sign up for it.

2. Illness or Death in the Family –> Emotional Pain
The doctor did not diagnose the symptoms in time and now it is too late to help your family member. The bad news has broken your heart. Grieving the loss of a loved one takes at least three years.

3. Your Partner Breaks Up with You –> Emotional Pain
Your partner has been cheating on you and you find out by walking in on them accidentally. You are in a state of shock. This pain takes years to heal. You may even be scarred for life and unable to love again.

4. You Get Fired from Your Job –> Emotional Pain
Your boss doesn't care that your parent died and if you take the day off to go to the funeral, you're fired. You go to the funeral and start looking for a new job. You will completely recover from this kind of setback.

DO NOT START POPPING THOSE VACUOUS PILLS FOR DEPRESSION

WHY?

Because all medications have side effects and you will find that you will now be suffering from your emotional pain and from the side effects of these medications. These pills are also dangerous because when you feel emotional pain, you keep popping the pills, like candy, overdose, and die. Prescription drugs are more dangerous than illegal drugs. These pills mask your emotional pain, and will not help you to grieve your losses and heal.

FEEL TO HEAL

When you feel pain, go into a private area and cry out your emotional pain and grief for hours, weeks, days, or years. The loss of a loved one can evoke tears for years to come, and you need to let the pain rise to the surface and be released. The day will come when the grief is over, and you will regain your vitality and zest for life.

DO NOT GIVE YOUR POWER AWAY

Do not give your power away to the people who come into your life and cause you pain. Here is a mantra that will help you change course and keep you on track for personal and professional success in school and in the real world.

"The First Day It's Crazy, Is The First Day It's Over"

Sharon Esther Lampert
Pr**odig**y, Prophet, Philosopher, and Poet

RED FLAGS OF DOOM AND GLOOM

Pay attention to the **Red Flags** of doom and gloom and heed their warnings. Everything in life has an expiration date.

Red Flag: Your teacher's assignments are insane. For example: Write a paper that covers the 12-18th century and examine the political, religious, cultural, and social changes that occurred. In this case, it is best to write an anonymous letter to the dean and the teacher, attach the ridiculous assignment, and let the dean and teacher work it out on their own.

Red Flag: Your partner is no longer interested in you. For example: Your partner no longer uses the pronoun "we" with regard to planning for the future. It is time to let go of this relationship and find a new love.

Red Flag: Your employer is having a business setback and will have to fire some employees to stay afloat. It is time to start looking for a new part-time job.

TOTAL RECALL: ACE EVERY TEST EVERY TIME

Manage Your Test Anxiety

1. Manage Your Time (CH 1)
- SMARTGRADES Academic Planner (fully loaded)
- Write a **DAILY ACTION PLAN**
- Manage Your Multiple Schedules

2. Take Control of the Academic Facts (CH 2)
For each class, you will have to manage 6 sets of facts:
Example:
English Class: 6 Sets of Facts
- Class notes & Test Review Notes
- Handouts & Test Review Notes
- Textbook & Test Review Notes

1 Folder: Homework Assignments, Quizzes, and Tests
Pocket 1. Homework Assignments
Pocket 2. Quizzes & Tests

E-Z: SMARTGRADES school notebooks contain class notes and test review notes in one notebook and 1000 learning tools

3. Eat Right and Sleep Well for Energy to Test (CH 3)
- High Fiber Breakfast: Oatmeal, Bran, Whole Grains
- Power Lunch (big plate): 1/4 Protein, 3/4 Vegetables
- Light Dinner (small plate): 1/4 Protein, 3/4 Vegetables
- Power Study Snacks: Fresh Fruits and Vegetables
- Avoid Processed Food full of Sugar, Salt, and Chemicals
- No Caffeine after 5 P.M. (poor sleep, tired next day)

4. Every Day Is Test Preparation Day (CH 5)

Study Periods: 45 minute study periods with 15 minute study breaks (stretch, eat study snack, and hydrate). Example:

English Study Period: 4-4:45 p.m.

- Read Actively (pencil in hand)
- Use the **SMARTGRADES SUCCESS STRATEGY** to process (absorb) facts for **Instant & Total Recall** to ace your test.
- Write Test-Review Notes: **Are You Test Ready?**
- Take a 15 Minute Study Break (stretch, eat a study snack, and hydrate (sugar free).

5. Test Day (CH 7)

- Review **Test Review Notes** to refresh your memory
- Practice positive Self-Talk: "My brain is the most powerful biological machine in the world, and I can ace any test!"
- Take deep breaths and exhale: worry, stress, and anxiety."

6. Manage Worry, Anxiety, and Stress That Can Escalate into Depression and Suicide

- Pay attention to the **RED FLAGS**, the warning signs.
- Disappointments cause pain, rage, and depression.
- **LIFE IS UNFAIR.** Everything in life has an expiration date.
- Do not take prescription pills with dangerous side effects that prop you up and mask your painful feelings.
- **FEEL TO HEAL.** Grieve your losses. Let the tears roll down your face for days, weeks, or even years.
- Change direction: lifestyle? friends? job?

SMARTGRADES SUCCESS STRATEGY
Every Student Earns an A Grade on the Next Test!
Every Student Is a Success Story!
Every Student Is Somebody Special!
Make the Grade & Achieve Your Dream!
Live Your Dreams!

Sharon Rose Sugar
The Paladin of Education for the 21st Century

What All Parents Need to Know About Their Child's Education
THIS BOOK SAVES LIVES
"The Silent Crisis Destroying America's Brightest Minds"
"Book of the Month" Alma Public Library, Wisconsin

Chapter 3

Are You Test Ready?
**SMARTGRADES
SUCCESS STRATEGY STUDY SKILLS**
Instant and Total Recall
Write Test Review Notes
Ace Your Test

SMARTGRADES
SUCCESS STRATEGY STUDY SKIILS

Step 1.   Estimation Tool
Step 2.   Divide and Conquer Tool
Step 3.   Active Reading Tool
Step 4.   Extraction Tool
Step 5.   Condensation Tool
Step 6.   Association Tool
Step 7.   Test Review Note Tool
Step 8.   Conversion Tool
Step 9.   Visualization Tool
Step 10. Self Test Tool

Don't Cram Facts for Short-Term Retention
Process Facts for Long-Term Retention

EARN A GRADE TODAY

Chapter 3

SMARTGRADES SUCCESS STRATEGY

Are You Test Ready?

Education is food for the brain. Students spend the entire day eating facts and building their brain muscles. If I give you a sandwich to eat, you cannot stuff the entire sandwich into your mouth. You have to take small bites and chew, chew, chew, and digest. Eating facts is like eating a sandwich. You have to take small amounts of information and chew (in-depth comprehension), chew (long-term retention), and chew (mastery of academic material).

Right after every class, go directly to your study area and write your **Test-Review Notes** to process (absorb) the facts for Instant & Total Recall to ace your exams.

DAILY ACTION PLAN
- ☑ 1. Get up early enough eat a fiber-fuel breakfast
- ☑ 2. Preread textbook chapter for maximum absorption
- ☑ 3. Go to class to receive teacher's wisdom and experience
- ☑ 4. Go to a well equipped study room (no distractions)
- ☑ 5. Use **SMARTGRADES SUCCESS STRATEGY** to process facts for Instant & Total Recall to ace your tests
- ☑ 6. Write three sets of **Test Review Notes** for (1) class notes, (2) handouts, and (3) textbook notes
- ☑ 7. Take a study break: Stretch, eat a study snack.
- ☑ 8. Set a regular bedtime for the energy to learn.

TOTAL RECALL: ACE EVERY TEST EVERY TIME

SMARTGRADES SUCCESS STRATEGY

To ace your exams, you have to develop three critical skills:

RETENTION, RECOGNITION, RECALL

1. **RETENTION** is your ability to absorb the facts.

2. **RECOGNITION** is reading the test question and knowing the answer.

3. **INSTANT RECALL** is popping out an answer in a jiffy.

4. **TOTAL RECALL** is long-term retention of all of the facts.

To acquire these 3 skills, you need **REVIEW** and **REPETITION**.

Here Are the 5 R's of Test Preparation
REVIEW, REPETITION, RETENTION, RECOGNITION, RECALL

The academic facts have to be processed (absorption) for **Instant & Total Recall** to ace your test. You have to eat facts, just like you eat food. The facts have to be digested. **SMARTGRADES SUCCESS STRATEGY** is a 10 step learning tool for **Instant & Total Recall** of the facts. Let's define each of the following terms:

Step 1.   Estimation Tool
Step 2.   Divide and Conquer Tool
Step 3.   Active Reading Tool
Step 4.   Extraction Tool
Step 5.   Condensation Tool
Step 6.   Association Tool
Step 7.   Test Review Note Tool
Step 8.   Conversion Tool
Step 9.   Visualization Tool
Step 10. Self-Test Tool

Step 1. Estimation Tool
Every paragraph contains one main idea and many supporting details. If you have ten paragraphs, then you have ten main ideas.

Step 2. Divide and Conquer Tool
You have to process one paragraph at a time for **Instant & Total Recall.** You cannot stuff a whole sandwich into your mouth. You have to take small bites, chew, chew, chew, and digest.

Step 3. Active Reading Tool
When you read, you need to be holding a pencil like a fisherman holds a net over the water to capture a fish. You are fishing for the facts. Every fact is a test question.

Step 4. Extraction Tool
You job is to extract the main idea and supporting details of every paragraph: Who, What, Where, When, and Why.

Step 5. Condensation Tool
Your job is to condense the facts and make them easier to digest, absorb, and process for Instant & Total Recall.

Step 6. Association Tool
Association links the unknown fact to a known fact in your mind. This is the glue that makes the facts stick to you.

Step 7. Test Review Note Tool
Your class notes, handouts, and textbook have to be processed for Instant & Total Recall to ace your tests.

Step 8. Conversion Tool
The facts have to be converted into test questions.

Step 9. Visualization Tool
Q: What type of test question is best suited for the facts?

Step 10. Self-Testing Tool
You have to answer your test questions to make sure that you have Instant & Total Recall and can ace your tests.

TOTAL RECALL: ACE EVERY TEST EVERY TIME

How to Process (Absorb) the Facts to Ace a Test

Tools of the Trade

SMARTGRADES
SUCCESS STRATEGY STUDY SKILLS

Steps to Success

Step 1. Gather Study Materials and Go to Study Area
- ☐ a. Class Notes
- ☐ b. Handouts
- ☐ c. Textbook

Step 2. Choose a Great Study Area
- ☐ a. No external distractions
- ☐ b. Good lighting
- ☐ c. Comfortable chair
- ☐ d. Big desk to hold all school supplies

Step 3. Clear Your Mind of Internal Negative Distractions
a. Worry and Anxiety: "I feel overwhelmed by workload!"
b. Fear of Failure: "I feel inadequate ... I can't keep up!"
c. Negative Self-Talk: "I am not smart enough...!"

Step 4. Develop Positive Self-Talk to Build Your Self-Esteem
a. "I have the power to make my dreams come true!"
b. "I have the power to transform weakness into strength!"
c. "I have the power to change bad habits into good habits!"

Step 5. Develop a Regular Study Period Schedule

Q1. Where do I study best:

❏ At Home ❏ In the Library ❏ Somewhere Else

Q2. When do I study best:

❏ In the Morning ❏ Afternoon ❏ Evening

Q3. How do I study best:

❏ Alone ❏ With a Friend ❏ In a Group

Q4. I need to take a break:

❏ Every 30 Minutes ❏ Every Hour ❏ Every Two Hours

Example: Regular Study Period Schedule

M:	CLASS	STUDY PERIOD	EXERCISE	STUDY PERIOD
T:	CLASS	STUDY PERIOD	EXERCISE	STUDY PERIOD
W:	CLASS	STUDY PERIOD	EXERCISE	STUDY PERIOD
T:	CLASS	STUDY PERIOD	EXERCISE	STUDY PERIOD
F:		Study:10-3 p.m.		
S:			Study:12-3 p.m.	
S:				Study:1-4 p.m.

Step 6. Plan Regular Study Periods Plan with Study Breaks

Study for 45 minutes and then take a 15 minute study break:

2-2:45	15 minute break	Write Class Notes Test Review Notes
3-3:45	15 minute break	Write Textbook Test Review Notes
4-4:45	15 minute break	Write Handout Test Review Notes
5-5:45	15 minute break	Write Rough Draft of Essay Paper
6-6:45	15 minute break	Do Math Homework

TOTAL RECALL: ACE EVERY TEST EVERY TIME

Step 7. Right After Class, Write Your Test Review Notes

SMARTGRADES SUCCESS STRATEGY

SMARTGRADES 1. Estimation Tool
Q1. How Many Main Ideas?
Every paragraph contains one main idea and many supporting details. If you have ten paragraphs, then you have ten main ideas.

Example: Estimate Main Ideas
1 main idea per paragraph
10 paragraphs = 10 main ideas

Paragraph 1
Main Idea:

Paragraph 2
Main Idea:

Paragraph 3
Main Idea:

_____

SMARTGRADES 2. Divide and Conquer Tool
You have to process one paragraph at a time for **Instant & Total Recall.** You cannot stuff a whole sandwich into your mouth. You have to take small bites, chew, chew, chew, and digest.

Paragraph 1
Main Idea:
Supporting Details:
Condense Facts:
Association Cue for Instant & Total Recall:
Sample Test Question:

SMARTGRADES BRAIN POWER REVOLUTION

SMARTGRADES 3. Active Reading Tool
When you read, you need to be holding a pencil like a fisherman holds a net over the water to capture a fish. You are fishing for the facts. Every fact is a test question. Underline the <u>main idea</u> and <u>supporting details.</u>

Example: Underline Main Idea and Supporting Details
<u>Thomas Jefferson</u> was an intellectual, statesman, and <u>third president of the United States.</u> Although Jefferson served as <u>governor of Virginia, ambassador to France, secretary of state, vice president, and president,</u> he is remembered in history less for the offices he held than for what he stood for.

SMARTGRADES 4. Extraction Tool
You job is to extract the main idea and supporting details of every paragraph: Who, What, Where, When, and Why.

Example: Extract Facts
<u>Thomas Jefferson</u> was an intellectual, statesman, and <u>third president of the United States.</u> Although Jefferson served as <u>governor of Virginia, ambassador to France, secretary of state, vice president, and president,</u> he is remembered in history less for the offices he held than for what he stood for.

One Main Idea   Many Supporting Details

Main Idea: Thomas Jefferson, 3rd President of U.S.A.

Many Supporting Details:
- Held many offices
- President
- Vice President
- Ambassador
- Secretary of State

TOTAL RECALL: ACE EVERY TEST EVERY TIME

SMARTGRADES 5. Condensation Tool
Your job is to condense the facts and make them easier to digest, absorb, and process for **Instant & Total Recall**.

Many Supporting Details:
- Held many offices
- President
- Vice President
- Ambassador
- Secretary of State

Example:Condense Facts
Held Many Offices = P/VP/AM/SS

SMARTGRADES 6. Association Tool for Instant & Total Recall
Association links the unknown fact to a known fact in your mind. Choose the Association Cue that works best for you. Personal memory is the most powerful Association Cue.

Example: Associate Facts
P/VP/AM/SS = Association Cue = Personal Memory

My Personal Association Cue Is:
PVP played on AM radio on weekends (Sat, Sun)
Totally ridiculous memory cue, but it works for me

SMARTGRADES 7. Test Review Note Tool
Your class notes, handouts, and textbook have to be processed for Instant & Total Recall to ace your tests.
- ☐ a. Test-Review Note for Class Notes
- ☐ b. Test-Review Note for Handouts
- ☐ c. Test-Review Note for Textbook Chapter

SMARTGRADES BRAIN POWER REVOLUTION

My Test-Review Note
Main Idea:
Supporting Details:
Condense Facts:
Association Cue for Instant & Total Recall:
Possible Test Question

SMARTGRADES 8 & 9: Visualization and Conversion Tool
Visualize test question and convert facts, the main idea, and supporting details into a sample test question.

Q. What type of test question is best suited for the facts?

Sample Test Question
Q. What positions did Thomas Jefferson hold?
(a) 3rd President of U.S.A.
(b) Governor of Virginia
(c) Ambassador to France
(d) Secretary of State U.S.A.
(e) Vice President of U.S.A.
(g) All of the Above

SMARTGRADES 10. Self-Testing Tool for Instant & Total Recall
To ace a test, you need to process (absorb) the facts for long term retention. Cramming facts for short-term retention does not work because you won't have Instant & Total Recall of the facts and you will not ACE your test.

Q1. Can you recall the facts in a jiffy for Instant Recall?
Q2. Can you recall all of the facts for Total Recall?

If you can't remember the fact, change the association cue.

SMARTGRADES PROCESSING TOOLS to Write Test-Review Notes
My Time Log:
Estimate (Fantasy): 5 Hours
Actual (Reality):
Error:
Speedbumps: Delays, Detours, or Distractions?

How to Associate Facts for Instant & Total Recall

The facts have to be processed for **Instant & Total Recall** to ace your test. To process the facts for long-term retention, you have to link the **UNKNOWN** fact to a **KNOWN** fact in your mind. This linking process is called Association.
For example, here are two unknown words:

Yin   Yang

One of these words is male and the other word is female. The word Yang is male. To process the fact for **Instant & Total Recall** — we want to associate the fact, that is link the **unknown** fact to a **known** fact in our mind.

Association

Unknown Fact	LINK	**Known** Fact in Mind
Yan**g** (male)	LINK	"g looks like a penis"

The letter "g' on the Yang looks like a male penis. You will remember this fact in an Instant and you will remember this for a lifetime. We linked the **unknown** fact to a **known** fact in your mind. This is how to achieve **Instant & Total Recall** of the facts.

Steps to Success

Step 1. Selection
Select facts to memorize: Main ideas and Supporting Details (who, what, where, when why, and how).

Step 2. Association
Choose the association cue that fits your learning style.

Acronym Cue: Use letters to condense the key facts. For example, to remember how to shoot a rifle, use the classic acronym BRASS, which stands for: Breath, Relax, Aim, Sight, Squeeze.

Acrostic Cue: Use a sentence to condense the key facts. For example, to remember the order of G-clef notes on sheet music, (E, G, B, D, F) use the classic acrostic: Every Good Boy Deserves Fun.

Rhyme Cue: Use rhymes to link the key facts together. For example, the classic, "I before E, except after C."

Music Cue: Make up a song or poem with the information in it. Sing the song or recite the poem several times.

Chaining Cue: Create a story where each word or idea you have to remember cues the next idea you need to recall. Use your imagination. If you had to remember the name, Shirley Temple, you could rhyme Shirley with curly and remember that she had curly hair around her temples.

Funny Cue: Write a joke that contains the key facts. The funniest, most outlandish, and the strangest concoction of memory cues makes memorizing easy.

TOTAL RECALL: ACE EVERY TEST EVERY TIME

SMARTGRADES SUCCESS STRATEGY

My Test-Review Notes to Ace the Test

Paragraph 1
- Extract Facts:
  Main Idea:
  Supporting Details:
  a.
  b.
  c.

- Condense Facts:
- Associate Facts:
- Convert to Test Question:
  Q. Who, What, Where, When, Why, How?

- Self-Test for Instant and Total Recall

Paragraph 2
- Extract Facts:
  Main Idea:
  Supporting Details:
  a.
  b.
  c.

- Condense Facts:
- Associate Facts:
- Convert to Test Question:
  Q. Who, What, Where, When, Why, How?

- Self-Test for Instant and Total Recall

SMARTGRADES BRAIN POWER REVOLUTION

Paragraph 3
- Extract Facts:
  Main Idea:
  Supporting Details:
  a.
  b.
  c.

- Condense Facts:
- Associate Facts:
- Convert to Test Question:
  Q. Who, What, Where, When, Why, How?

- Self-Test for Instant and Total Recall

Paragraph 4
- Extract Facts:
  Main Idea:
  Supporting Details:
  a.
  b.
  c.

- Condense Facts:
- Associate Facts:
- Convert to Test Question:
  Q. Who, What, Where, When, Why, How?

- Self-Test for Instant and Total Recall

University Grading Systems

DEPT OF STATISTICS:
All grades are plotted along the Normal (Gaussian) curve.

DEPT OF PSYCHOLOGY:
Students are asked to blot ink in their exam books, close them, and turn them in. The professor opens the books and assigns the first grade that comes to mind.

DEPT OF HISTORY:
All students get the same grade they got last year.

DEPT OF RELIGION:
Grade is determined by God.

DEPT OF PHILOSOPHY:
What is a grade?

LAW SCHOOL:
Students are asked to defend their position of why they should receive an A.

What Different Degrees Mean

The graduate with a science degree asks,
"Why does it work?"

The graduate with an engineering degree asks,
"How does it work?"

The graduate with a management degree asks,
"How much will it cost?"

The graduate with an arts degree asks,
"Do you want fries with that?"

When You Take a Test, You Are Really Being Tested on Two Things:

How Much You Know About the Subject

How Much You Know About Taking a Test

Chapter 6
How to Ace Every Test Every Time

He Who Asks a Question Is
a Fool for Five Minutes.
He Who Does Not Ask a Question
Remains a Fool Forever

Chinese Proverb

Chapter 7

Ace Your Test

Tools of the Trade

The Day the Test Is Announced
Two Weeks Before the Test
The Night Before the Test
The Day of the Test

Steps to Success

Step 1. The Day the Test is Announced, Ask Questions

Q1. What subjects are on the test?
Q2. What subjects are not on the test?
Q3. What are the most important subjects?
Q4. What are the least important subjects?
Q5. What is the format of the test?
Q6. How many questions are on the test?
Q7. How is the test scored?
Q8. How does the test count toward percentage of grade?
Q9. Is there a penalty for guessing?
Q10. Are there sample exams on file in the library?
Q11. Is the test cumulative?

Step 2. Two Weeks Before the Test

Two weeks before the test, start reviewing your **Test Review Notes** to check to see that you processed the academic facts for **Instant & Total Recall** to ace your test.

Example

Priority 1. Start Reviewing **Test Review Notes**

Priority 2. Do Homework Assignments

Priority 3. Write Papers

Priority 4. Proofread Written Work

Priority 5. Preread Textbook Chapter

Example: DAILY ACTION PLAN

Priority 1. Review Test Review Notes for Test in 2 Weeks

a. Self-Test for Instant Recall

b. Self-Test for Total Recall

c. Change weak Association Cues that do not work well

d. Visit a tutoring center if you are still feeling confused and need further clarification of the academic facts

Priority 2. Do Homework Assignments Due Tomorrow

a. Math, Chapter 4, Problems 4,5,6

b. Science, Chapter 3, Questions 7, 8

Priority 3. Write English Essay Due Friday

a. Choose researchable topic

b. Use encyclopedia for general overview of topic

c. List experts in the field

d. List primary and secondary source materials

e. List pro and con arguments

f. Write "Thesis Statement," state your point of view

g. Write "Outline" of main ideas and supporting details

h. Visit teacher's office for approval of essay "Outline"

i. Write Rough Draft, "Writing Is Rewriting!"

j. Write Final Draft

Priority 4. Proofread All Written Work to Perfection

- Proofread for spelling, grammar, and punctuation
- Enlarge text to font 22 to be able to see clearly
- Use computer spellchecker
- Use computer software to read text aloud
    a. Text Edit software
    b. Adobe Acrobat software
- Use your **SMARTGRADES** Proofreading Tools (see book, **EVERY DAY, AN EASY A**)

Priority 5. Preread Textbook Chapter for Class

- Read the end-of-chapter summary for main ideas

Step 3. The Night Before the Test

- Review Test-Review Notes for Instant & Total Recall

- Prepare pens, pencils, sharpener, calculator, tissues, and watch and place in pencil case

- Prepare your clothing, matching shirt, pants, and socks

- Don't drink caffeine after 5 p.m. (tea, soda, coffee)

- Get 8 hours of deep sleep to feel energized

- Set your alarm clock

Step 4. The Day of the Test

- Wake up early enough to eat a nutritious breakfast

  Example:
  Breakfast of Champions: oatmeal, maple syrup, cinnamon, sliced apples, and walnuts, and hydrate

- Review Test Review Notes to refresh your memory

- Manage Your Test Anxiety
  Anxiety and stress are debilitating. They will ZAP your energy and destroy your ability to focus and concentrate on the test and you will draw blanks. Practice deep breathing exercises to be able to maintain a calm composure.

Example
The 3-Breath Method of Relaxation Breathing
- Get in a comfortable position, spine straight, feet flat on the floor. Close your eyes.
- Concentrate on your body, and notice where there is tension, discomfort or stress.
- Take a deep breath, visualize all your stress, then breathe out. While breathing out, visualize all the stress leaving your body.
- Repeat these steps at least three times.

- **Develop Your Self-Esteem with Positive Self-Talk**

Q. When you listen to your inner voice, do you hear positive supportive messages, e.g., "I have the strength to make my dreams come true." On a daily basis, you need to develop your self-esteem with positive self-talk.

Examples:
- Fear is only a feeling; it cannot hold me back!

- I know that my potential is unlimited!

- I have the strength to make my dreams come true!

- I am proud of myself for even daring to try!

- I grow in strength with every forward step I take!

- I release my hesitation and make room for victory!

TOTAL RECALL: ACE EVERY TEST EVERY TIME

Step 5. The Test Begins

1. The Instructions:
First, listen carefully to oral instructions and then read all written instructions.

2. The Test Begins:
Jot down in the corner of the test everything you may forget during the test.

Example: Jot Down Facts on Scrap Paper
Main Idea:
Supporting Example:
Expert in Field:
Pro Argument:
Con Argument:
Add: Analysis. Use **SMARTGRADES** Critical Thinking Tools (p.119) e.g., Separate facts from belief systems and opinions

3. The Time:
Budget your time. Do not linger over difficult questions.

4. Your Mental, Emotional, and Spiritual Focus:
Concentrate on what you do know, don't worry about what you don't know.

5. The Question:

- Answer the questions you know first.
- Concentrate on one question at a time.
- Read each question completely before you begin to answer it.
- Answer question asked, not the one you may have expected.
- Go back to the ones you did not answer.
- Don't linger over difficult questions.
- Recall of the information you need may be triggered by completing other questions.

6. The Answer:

- Write down answer before reading choices.
- Read your answer choices carefully.
- Eliminate the choices that are clearly implausible.
- Don't search for hidden or extra meanings.
- Compare similarities & differences between choices.

Examine each word in answer for true or false possibility.
Key Words: All, Only, Always, Because = Generally False
Key Words: Few, Many, Much, Often, Many, Some, Perhaps, Generally = Possibly True
Break down complex sentences into smaller parts.
If small phrase = false, then entire statement = false.
If each word = false; then entire statement = false.

Change answers if you have a reason for doing so.
However do not change your answers based on a whim.
Use all the time allowed. If you finish early, proofread your paper for errors.

The More You Understand, The Less You Have to Remember

Craig A. McCraw

Chapter 7
Ace Your Test

"If any one faculty of our nature may be called more wonderful than the rest, I do think it is memory. There seems something more speakingly incomprehensible in the powers, the failures, the inequalities of memory, than in any other of our intelligences. The memory is sometimes so retentive, so serviceable, so obedient; at others, so bewildered and so weak; and at others again, so tyrannic, so beyond control! We are, to be sure, a miracle every way; but our powers of recollecting and of forgetting do seem peculiarly past finding out."

Jane Austen

Chapter 7

Ace Your Test

Tools of the Trade

Multiple Choice Exams

Essay Exams

True False Exams

Matching Exams

Fill in the Blank Exams

Open Book Exams

Take Home Exams

Oral Exams

Standardized Exams

Steps to Success

Step 1. Prepare for the Test the Teacher Will Give

a. Essay Exam: Answer the question asked

b. Multiple Choice Exam: The answer is right in front of you

c. Oral Exam: Prepare for a personal interview format

d. Take Home Test: Use **SMARTGRADES** Critical Thinking Tools for in-depth analysis of academic material (p.119)

TOTAL RECALL: ACE EVERY TEST EVERY TIME

How to Ace Your Multiple Choice Test

Steps to Success

Step 1. Answer the easy questions first to build your confidence.

Step 2. Underline the key words in the question and try to answer the question. These tests rely on recognition, rather than recall.

Step 3. Think of multiple choice answers as a series of true or false statements. Read all of the choices even if the first choice seems correct. Compare similarities and differences between choices.

Step 4. Circle the absolute words in the question and the answer.

The absolutes are: all, none, always, never, only. These absolute words usually indicate a false choice.

Step 5. Circle the negative words in the question and the answer. Circle the negative words: not or except. These confusing questions cause careless errors. Mark each option with a T or F. Usually you are looking for a true statement. In this case, you are looking for a false statement.

Step 6. Find the dumb and dumber choices in the answer Cross out the two choices that are dumb and dumber. Examine the question and answer for clues.

Step 7. Change an answer when you have an intelligent reason to do so.

Beware the Dangers of Answer Sheets

Answer sheets allow exams to be scanned and marked automatically. Here are common mistakes to avoid:

1. Remember to record your name and student number on the actual answer sheet.

2. Use pencil so you can correct mistakes.

3. Do not cross out a mistake and mark another answer because the scanner will read this as "two" responses and record it as incorrect.

4. Always check your answers with the right question.

5. Consider marking your answers first on the exam paper, then transferring them to the answer sheet.

TOTAL RECALL: ACE EVERY TEST EVERY TIME

How to Ace Your Essay Test

Steps to Success

Step 1. Underline Key Word to Answer Question Asked

ANALYZE — Find the main ideas and show how they are related and why they are important.

COMMENT ON — Discuss, criticize, or explain its meaning as completely as possible.

COMPARE — Show both the similarities and differences.

CONTRAST — Show the differences.

CRITICIZE — Give your judgment or reasoned opinion of something, showing its good and bad points. It is not necessary to attack it.

DEFINE — Give the formal meaning by distinguishing it from related terms. This is often a matter of giving a memorized definition.

DESCRIBE — Write a detailed account or verbal picture in a logical sequence or story form.

DIAGRAM — Make a graph, chart, drawing. Be sure you label it and add a brief explanation if it is needed.

DISCUSS — Describe giving the details and explaining the pros and cons of it.

ENUMERATE — Name and list the main ideas one by one. Number them.

EVALUATE — Give your opinion or some expert's opinion of the truth or importance of the concept. Tell the advantages and disadvantages.

ILLUSTRATE — Explain or make it clear by concrete examples, comparison, or analogies.

INTERPRET — Give the meaning using examples and personal comments to make it clear.

JUSTIFY — Give a statement of why you think it is so. Give reasons for your statement or conclusion.

LIST — Produce a numbered list of words, sentences, or comments. Same as enumerate.

OUTLINE — Give a general summary. It should contain a series of main ideas supported by secondary ideas. Omit minor details. Show the organization of the ideas.

PROVE — Show by argument or logic that it is true. The word prove has a very special meaning in mathematics and physics.

RELATE — Show the connections between things, telling how one causes or is like another.

TOTAL RECALL: ACE EVERY TEST EVERY TIME

REVIEW – Give a survey or summary in which you look at the important parts and criticize where needed.

STATE – Describe the main points in precise terms. Be formal. Use brief, clear sentences. Omit details or examples.

SUMMARIZE – Give a brief, condensed account of the main ideas. Omit details and examples.

TRACE – Follow the progress or history of the subject.

Step 2. Restate Question as Introductory Sentence
Read the essay question and restate the question as the introductory sentence of your essay and add on the facts.

Example
Q. What are the most important issues your field is facing today?

A. The most important issues that my field is facing today are: Add main idea and major and minor details.

Step 3. Jot Down Main Ideas and Supporting Details
Jot down in the corner of the test the main ideas and supporting details to organize your thoughts before you write down the answer.

Main Ideas:
1.
2.
3.

Main Idea 1:
Supporting Details:
1. Expert in Field:
2. Indirect Quote:
3. Example:
4. Analysis:
5. Sum It Up:

Main Idea 2:
Supporting Details:
1. Expert in Field:
2. Indirect Quote:
3. Example:
4. Analysis:
5. Sum It Up:

Main Idea 3:
Supporting Details:
1. Expert in Field:
2. Indirect Quote:
3. Example:
4. Analysis:
5. Sum It Up:

Step 4. Use Standard Essay Structure
Use Introduction, Body, and Conclusion

Step 5. Use Standard Paragraph Structure

Sentence 1. Restate essay question ...

Sentence 2. According to Expert... (add quote)

Sentence 3. For example ... (proof)

Sentence 4. As a result ... (analysis)

Sentence 5. In conclusion ... (sum it up)

Step 6. Proofread Paper to Perfection
Proofread for spelling, punctuation, grammar, and neatness.

TOTAL RECALL: ACE EVERY TEST EVERY TIME

How to Ace Your True False Exam

Steps to Success

Step 1. Examine the Sentence
Every part of a true sentence must be "true." If any one part of the sentence is false, the whole sentence is false despite many other true statements. Long sentences often include groups of words set off by punctuation. Pay attention to the "truth" of each of these phrases. If one is false, it usually indicates a "false" answer.

Step 2. Underline Key Words
Pay close attention to negatives, qualifiers, absolutes, and long strings of statements.

Negatives: "No, Not, Cannot"
Qualifiers: "Sometimes, Often, Frequently, Ordinarily,
Absolutes: : "No, never, none, always, every, entirely, only"

Step 3. Guess True If You Are Unsure
Often true/false tests contain more true answers than false answers. You have more than 50% chance of being right with "true."

How to Ace Your Matching Exam

Steps to Success

Step 1. Use a Light Pencil

Mark them lightly with a pencil until you are completely done.

Step 2. Start with Matches that You Know Instantly

Step 3. Use a Darker Pencil

Make a second pass through matches, mark matches you are absolutely sure of with a darker penciled line.

Step 4. Search for Clues

Look for clues or relationships in the matches you aren't 100% sure of that you didn't think of the first time.

Step 5. Search for Other Possibilities

Look for another phrase that can be used instead of your first choice.

TOTAL RECALL: ACE EVERY TEST EVERY TIME

How to Ace Your Fill in the Blank Exam

Steps to Success

Step 1. This Exam Is Most Difficult and Most Feared
You have to have the answers, such as names, places, and dates memorized for **Instant & Total Recall**.

Step 2. SMARTGRADES SUCCESS STRATEGY
Use the new learning technology, **SMARTGRADES SUCCESS STRATEGY** to process (absorb) the facts for **Instant & Total Recall** and ace the test.

Step 3. Answer the Easy Questions First

Step 4. Underline the Key Words in the Question

Step 5. Other Questions May Jog Your Memory
Sometimes answers to questions you don't know are supplied in other questions.

Step 6. Guessing
The chances of getting a correct answer by writing down a wild guess is very slim, although not entirely unlikely.

How to Ace Your True False Exam

Steps to Success

Step 1. Examine the Sentence

Every part of a true sentence must be "true." If any one part of the sentence is false, the whole sentence is false, despite many other true statements. Long sentences often include groups of words set off by punctuation. Pay attention to the "truth" of each of these phrases. If one is false, it usually indicates a "false" answer.

Step 2. Underline Key Words

Pay close attention to negatives, qualifiers, absolutes, and long strings of statements.

Negatives: "No, Not, Cannot"
Qualifiers: "Sometimes, Often, Frequently, Ordinarily,
Absolutes: "No, never, none, always, every, entirely, only"

Step 3. Guess True If You Are Unsure

Often true/false tests contain more true answers than false answers. You have more than 50% chance of being right with "true."

How to Ace Your Open Book Exam

Steps to Success

Step 1. Use Textbook and Test Review Notes
Since you have already condensed the facts from your textbook into Test Review Notes, they are probably the fastest way to access the facts.

Step 2. Use Standard Essay Format
a. Write in complete sentences.
b. Restate the essay question as the introductory sentence and add on the facts.
c. Use an Introduction, Body, and Conclusion
d. Use transition words to bridge ideas:

Sentence 1. On one hand ... (the Pro argument)
　　　　　　　On the other hand ... (the Con argument)
Sentence 2. According to expert... (add quote)
Sentence 3. For example ...
Sentence 4. As a result ... (analysis)
Sentence 5. In conclusion ... (sum it up)

Step 3. Proofread to Perfection
Check for spelling, grammar, punctuation, and neatness.

How to Ace Your Take Home Exam

Steps to Success

Step 1. What Kinds of Material Can Be Used?
Take Home Exams are unrestricted. The main restriction for **Take Home Exams** is that they must be your work — you must attempt them by yourself without any help from others.

Step 2. What Do Take Home Exams Test?
They don't test your memory. They test your ability to find and use information for problem solving, and to deliver well-structured and well-presented arguments and solutions. They require you to apply knowledge rather than just remember facts.

Step 3. Follow the Instructions for Open Book Exams

Step 4. Use SMARTGRADES CRITICAL THINKING TOOLS
To give a comprehensive analysis of the academic material, apply the **SMARTGRADES** Critical Thinking Tools. Separate facts from belief systems and opinions of author.

What Is the Hardest Task in the World?

To Think

Ralph Waldo Emerson

Critical Thinking Tools
For Take Home Tests

The Trouble with the World
Is that the Stupid Are Cocksure and
the Intelligent Are Full of Doubt

Bertrand Russell

THERE IS ONLY ONE
TRUTH
NO ONE HAS THE TRUTH

Philosopher Queen Sharon Esther Lampert

Aristotle's Topoi

1. Use Definition
2. Explore Relationship
3. Examine Circumstance
4. Rely on Testimony

Chapter 10
Critical Thinking Tools

Tools of the Trade

1. Read with an Open Mind
2. Read with a Critical Mind
3. Evaluate the Underlying Assumptions
4. Read for Arguments Based on Fallacies
5. Read for Inductive and Deductive Reasoning

Steps to Success

Step 1. Read with an Open Mind
Develop mental flexibility, a willingness to think clearly and weigh all sides of every question. To resolve a problem, attack a problem with an open mind. Prepare to consider all possibilities and probe the issue to the heart.

Step 2. Read with a Critical Mind
Separate the facts of the story (verifiable evidence) from the opinions of the author. Caution: Some facts, such as statistical surveys and historical events are based on "opinions."

Step 3. Evaluate the Underlying Assumptions
Assumptions are the set of belief systems that are considered to be self-evident.

Step 4. Read for Arguments Based on Fallacies
Learn to recognize the presentation of misleading evidence that is false.

Misdirected Appeals: Appeal to authority, appeal to common or popular belief, appeal to common practice or tradition, appeal to indirect consequences, appeal to wishful thinking.

Emotional Appeals: Appeal to fear or scare tactics, appeal to force, appeal to loyalty or peer pressure, appeal to pity or sob story, appeal to prejudice, appeal to stereotypes, appeal to hatred, appeal to vanity.

Step 5. Read for Inductive and Deductive Reasoning
Induction argues from observation from the specific to the general. Deduction argues from the general to the specific (rules and laws).

A Checklist for Critical Thinking Tools

Q1. Did you read with an open mind?

Q2. Did you think clearly and weigh all sides of every question?

Q3. Did you resolve a problem, and attack a problem with a flexible mind?

Q4. Did you consider all possibilities and probe the issue to the heart?

Q5. Did you read with a critical mind and separate the facts of the story (verifiable evidence) from the opinions of the author.

Q6. Did you evaluate the underlying assumptions?

Q7. Did you read for arguments based on fallacies?

Misdirected Appeals:
1. Appeal to authority
2. Appeal to common or popular belief
3. Appeal to common practice or tradition
4. Appeal to indirect consequences
5. Appeal to wishful thinking

Emotional Appeals:
1. Appeal to fear or scare tactics
2. Appeal to force
3. Appeal to loyalty or peer pressure
4. Appeal to pity or sob story
5. Appeal to prejudice
6. Appeal to stereotypes
7. Appeal to hatred
8. Appeal to vanity

Q: Did you read for inductive and deductive reasoning?

How to Ace Your Oral Exam

Steps to Success

Step 1. Create a Good Impression
- Dress well and appropriately
- Turn off your cell phone
- Arrive at the location early
- Review Test Review Notes
- Practice positive self-talk: "I am the brightest banana in the bunch."

Step 2. Oral Exams Are Similar to Interviews
- Introduce yourself immediately and smile
- Give the instructor all of your attention
- Keep good posture and eye contact
- Stay focused through the exam
- Maintain your self-confidence and composure
- Be an intelligent listener as well as a talker
- Do not ramble if you do not know an answer
- If you do not know the answer, ask the teacher to ask the question in a different format to jog your memory
- Answer questions with more than "yes" or "no"
- Use two or three key points or examples to demonstrate your knowledge
- Thank the instructor

How to Transform an Exam Failure into a Success

You rushed through an exam, afraid that you will run out of time, and made careless mistakes:

- You misread the questions
- You misread the directions
- You blackened the wrong box on an answer sheet
- You skipped a question or two
- You forgot to write legibly

Steps to Success

Step 1. Ask for a Redo
An instructor may allow you to rewrite an essay exam, rework a math problem from the original question, and improve your grade. The worst they are going to say is no.

Step 2. Ask for Extra Credit Work
Ask for extra credit work to make up for a poor performance on a key exam.

Step 3. Review Mistakes
All knowledge bases are cumulative. Sometimes you get a problem wrong because you didn't understand the subject as well as you thought. After an exam fill in your knowledge gaps, to be prepared for the next test.

Step 4. Talk to Your Teacher
Ask your instructor for an explanation of your grade or comment. Use this as a time to find out how you can do better next time. Keep track of your strengths and weaknesses.

Standardized Exam Tools
How to Ace Your Verbal Analogy Exam

Steps to Success

Step 1. First, create a sentence in your mind that uses the two capitalized words.

Step 2. Learn to recognize common types of analogies.

Step 3. Eliminate answer pairs that are clearly wrong.

Step 4. Beware of possibly correct answers that appear in reverse order.

Step 5. If more than one choice appears possible, analyze the words again.

Step 6. Consider alternative meanings of words, as well as alternative parts of speech.

Step 7. If you don't know the meaning a word, try to recall if you've ever heard it in an expression. The context of the expression may suggest the meaning of the word.

Step 8. Beware of obvious answers. They may be there only to mislead you.

Standardized Exam Tools
How to Ace Your Verbal Antonyms Exam

Steps to Success

Step 1. Use word parts (prefixes, roots, suffixes) to figure out the probable meaning of unknown words.

Step 2. Be aware of secondary meanings of words. For example, 'appreciation' can just as readily mean 'increase' as it does 'gratitude'. When no answer seems correct, look for an alternative (or 'secondary') meaning for your antonym/opposite choice.

Step 3. Consider the 'feel' of the word. It may create a sense in you of its meaning, such as a word like 'grandiose'. It may have a positive or negative connotation, which may help you to eliminate some choices.

Step 4. Try to think of similarly constructed words that you may recognize and that may give you a clue as to the meaning of an otherwise unknown word.

Step 5. Think of a recognizable context for a word you don't recognize. Let the context of the word in a phrase or sentence suggest its probable meaning.

Stap 6. Think of an opposite meaning for the capitalized word, even before you look at the actual choices.

Step 7. Read all the choices before selecting your answer.

English is a funny language;
that explains why we park our car
in the driveway — and
drive our car on the parkway.

Unknown

How to Ace an English Test

How to Ace an English Test

Step 1. Choose a Great Book to Read
Read a book by your favorite author, read a book on your favorite subject, or read a famous or popular book.

Step 2. Increase Your Reading Rate
a. Read in a quiet place, free of external distractions (noise) and social interruptions (phone).
b. Before you begin reading, clear your mind of internal distractions (worry, anxiety, and stress).
c. To keep your focus and concentration, break down the big reading assignment into smaller manageable sizes.
d. To increase your reading rate, see more words, per line, per glance.
e. While reading, skip a hard word and finish the sentence.

Step 3. Increase Your Reading Comprehension
While reading, if questions arise, jot them down in the margins of the book.

Step 4. Read with a Purpose
As you read, keep a list of the significant facts in the story.
- Main Characters
- Minor Characters
- Quotations
- Relationships
- Dates

- Places
- Sequence of Events
- Main Conflict
- Author
- Social Issue
- Message of Book
- Background of the author (birthplace and date)
- Background of the book (time and place in history)
- Stylistic Features
- Narrative Strategies

Step 5. Read with a Critical Mind
Separate the facts of story from opinions of author.

Facts of Story	Opinions of Author
1.	
2.	
3.	

Step 6. Summarize the Chapters
After reading each chapter, summarize each chapter into 5-10 sentences.

Summary Chapter 1.

Summary Chapter 2.

Summary Chapter 3.

Step 7. The Point of View and Narrative Technique

Q. Who's telling the story?

Step 8. The Plot and Narrative Structure

Plot is what happens in a story, and structure is the order in which the novel presents the plot. Every plot and every story has an end as well as a beginning.

Q1. What effects does the ending have on the way we read a novel or other story?

Step 9. The Setting?

Q2. Where does the action take place?

The Chronological Setting:

Q3. What does setting a novel several decades earlier than the time of its writing and publication imply?

The Place:

Q4. Does the novel describe landscape, cities, and interiors in great detail?

Q5. What is the relation of a particular setting to a novel's main characters, and can you imagine them in a different setting.

Step 10. The Characterization

- Physical description – telling us what the character looks like

- Dialogue – what the character says

- Physical actions – what the character does (particularly in relation to what he or she says or thinks.)

- Thoughts, or metal actions – the character's inner life, what the character thinks

- Judgment by others – what other characters say and think about this fictional person

- The narrator's judgement – what narrator tells us about the character

- The author's judgement – what the author thinks of the character (sometimes difficult to determine until late in the narrative)

Step 11. The Theme vs. Subject

- The subject is the general topic or topics the book implicitly discusses.

- The theme is what the novel implies we should think about such subjects; it's what the book means.

Those Who Forget the Past
Are Condemned to Repeat It

George Santayana

How to Ace a History Test

TOTAL RECALL: ACE EVERY TEST EVERY TIME

How to Ace a History Test

Read with a Purpose
As you read, keep a list of the significant facts.
- Dates
- Places
- Sequence of Events
- People
- Map

Read with a Critical Mind
Read Primary Source Material (autobiographical)

Facts of Story   Opinions of Author
1.
2.
3.

Evaluate Primary Source Texts
1. Purpose of the Author
Q. What is the author's central claim?

2. Arguments to Achieve those Goals
Q. What are the steps in the argument?
Q. How is the author breaking down sub-points?

3. Values
Q. How might the difference between our values and the values of the author influence the way we understand the text?

4. Epistemology (evaluating truth content)
Q. How do you know what you know?
Q. What is the truth, and how is it determined?

Examine for Credible vs. Reliable Text

- Reliability refers to our ability to trust the consistency of the author's account of the truth.

- Credibility refers to our ability to trust the author's account of the truth on the basis of her or his tone and reliability.

Examine for Objective vs. Neutral Text

- Neutrality refers to the stake an author has in a text.

- Objectivity refers to an author's ability to convey the truth free of underlying values, cultural values, and biases.

Read Secondary Source Material (biographical)
Secondary sources are only the author's interpretation of past events. Different authors have different interpretations. If you read enough secondary sources you may begin to see differences. This will help you to form you own opinions.

Facts of Story   Opinions of Author
1.
2.
3.

> If I Create from the Heart,
> Nearly Everything Works;
> If from the Head Almost Nothing
>
> Marc Chagall

Critical Thinking	**Creative Thinking**
analytic	generative
convergent	divergent
vertical	lateral
probability	possibility
judgment	suspended judgment
focused	diffuse
objective	subjective
answer	answers
left brain	right brain
verbal	visual
linear	associative
reasoning	richness, novelty
yes but	yes and

How to Ace a Creative Arts Project

SEE THE WORLD THROUGH THE EYES OF A CREATIVE GENIUS

POETREE

Ink needs a pen.
Pen needs paper.
Paper needs a poem.
Poem needs a poet.
Poet needs a muse.
Muse needs a poet.
Poet needs divine inspiration.
Divine inspiration needs divine intervention.
Divine intervention needs divine grace.
Divine grace needs immortality.
Immortality needs eternity.
Eternity needs readers of poetry.

Sharon Esther Lampert
V.E.S.S.E.L. VERY. EXTRA. SPECIAL. SHARON. ESTHER. LAMPERT.

Please Handle My Poems Gently.
These Poems Are My Remains.

Sharon Esther Lampert

www.WorldFamousPoems.com
The Greatest Poems Ever Written on Extraordinary World Events

How to Ace a Creative Arts Project

WORLD PREMIERE!
Creative Thinking Tools

10 Tools of the Trade

1. V.E.S.S.E.L.
2. INSPIRATION
3. IMPREGNATION
4. INCUBATION
5. GENESIS
6. SILENT:LISTEN
7. METAMORPHOSIS
8. REVELATION
9. SIGNATURE
10. IMMORTALITY

Read: "Unleash The Creator, The God Within: 10 Esoteric Laws of Genius & Creativity"

Steps to Success

Step 1. V.E.S.S.E.L.
Keep an open mind and heart, so that you can receive inspirations that come from everywhere. Artistic gifts are inherited. There are good, great, and gifted **ARTISTS.**

Step 2. INSPIRATION
When something moves you emotionally, and transforms your inner world in such a way that you feel differently, think differently, and see differently — that external force is called inspiration. Inspiration is everywhere!

Step 3. IMPREGATION (ARTIST & ARTWORK BECOME ONE)
You are inspired and become impregnated with an idea.

Step 4. INCUBATION
The **ARTWORK** resides within the **ARTIST** and grows quietly over time. There is no such thing as "Writer's Block." It is a myth. You must be patient and allow **ARTWORK** to incubate within you.

Step 5. GENESIS (ARTIST & ARTWORK BECOME TWO)
When **ARTWORK** is ready to be born, it takes on a life of its own, separates from the **ARTIST**, and has its own destiny (mission, message, and meaning) e.g., music composition.

Step 6. SILENT: LISTEN
The **ARTIST** remains silent and listens within to the **ARTWORK**.

Step 7. METAMORPHOSIS: MISSION, MEANING, MESSAGE
The **ART** and the **ARTIST** are now two separate entities. The **ART** and the **ARTIST** have to be nurtured for both of them to grow and reach maturity.

Step 8. REVELATION: MESSAGE
The **ART** touches other people with its own message, and has its distinct own destiny, separate from the **ARTIST**.

Step 9. SIGNATURE
The **ART** bears the autograph of the **ARTIST**.

Step 10. IMMORTALITY
ARTWORK lives beyond the life of the **ARTIST**.
ARTIST IS MORTAL. ART IS IMMORTAL.

Steps to Success

Most creative people credit their vivid imaginations for their success, e.g., J.K. Rowling and Harry Potter.

Q1. Do you have the emotional, spiritual, and intellectual fortitude to express your ideas without fear from shame and ridicule?

Q2. Do you have a vivid imagination?

Q3. Do you write down your wild'n'crazy ideas and let them mature into a poem, a play, or a novel?

Q4. Are you a daydreamer? Do you write down your daydreams?

Q5. Do you let your mind flow freely to associate and brainstorm for ideas?

To Do List: Creative Idea Journal

Creative thinking requires thinking "outside the box." Start a creative ideas journal. List all ideas that come to mind, no matter how bizarre, weird, or strange, and see where they take you. Perhaps a novel will emerge, or a poem, or a plot for a movie script or even a play.

Theory Guides. Experiment Decides.

How to Ace a Science Test

How to Ace a Science Test

The scientific method is a process for experimentation that is used to explore observations that use the five senses, and to answer questions about the natural world. Scientists use the scientific method to search for cause and effect relationships in nature. An experiment is designed so that changes to one item cause something else to vary in a predictable way. The sciences rely heavily on numbers as data, and on replicable experimentation to measure and calculate results.

Tools of the Trade

The Scientific Method
- Make Observations By Using Your 5 Senses
- Ask Questions
- Perform Experiments
- Collect Data
- Measure Data
- Classify Data
- Make a Hypothesis
- Interpret Data
- Analyze Information
- Draw Conclusions
- Make a Prediction
- Verification of Experiment

The Science Report

Section 1.   Title Page
Section 2.   Abstract
Section 3.   Table of Contents
Section 4.   Question, Variables, and Hypothesis
Section 5.   Background Research
Section 6.   Materials List
Section 7.   Experimental Procedure
Section 8.   Data Analysis and Discussion
Section 9.   Conclusions
Section 10. Ideas for Future Research
Section 11. Acknowledgements
Section 12. Bibliography

Q: What Is Scientific Thinking?
Scientific (and critical) thinking is based on three things:
1. **Empiricism:** Using empirical evidence found in nature. Using evidence that is found in nature. It is evidence that is perceptible from the senses; evidence that one can see, hear, touch, taste, or smell.

2. **Rationalism:** Practicing logical reasoning

3. **Skepticism:** Possessing a skeptical attitude about presumed knowledge that leads to self-questioning, holding tentative conclusions, and being undogmatic (willingness to change one's beliefs).

TOTAL RECALL: ACE EVERY TEST EVERY TIME

How to Ace a Science Test

Learn the New Science Terminology

In every science lesson, new science concepts and big science vocabulary words are introduced. Spelling science words as well as pronouncing these words can be difficult. Not to worry, there will never be a spelling test of science vocabulary.

Take Organized Class Notes

Science Word: **Definition:**   **Draw a Picture:**
1.
2.
3.

Q1. What are the most important science concepts?
1.
2.
3.

Q2. What is the correct sequence of the science reaction?
1.
2.
3.

Understand the Fundamental Science Concepts:
- Systems, order, and organization
- Evidence, models, and explanations
- Change, constancy, and measurement
- Evolution and equilibrium
- Form and function

Science as Inquiry develops questioning and reasoning abilities. The processes associated with scientific inquiry include:
- Asking questions
- Planning and conducting investigations
- Using appropriate tools and techniques to gather data
- Thinking critically and logically about relationships between evidence and explanations
- Constructing and analyzing alternative explanations
- Communicating scientific arguments

Use your **SMARTGRADES SUCCESS STRATEGY** to memorize the science facts for **Instant & Total Recall** to ace your science test, as follows:

10 STEP SMARTGRADES SUCCESS STRATEGY
Step 1. Estimation
Step 2. Divide and Conquer
Step 3. Active Reading
Step 4. Extraction
Step 5. Condensation
Step 6. Association
Step 7. Test Review Notes
Step 8. Conversion
Step 9. Visualization
Step 10. Self-Test

WORLD PEACE EQUATION

VG+VL=VP

Virtue of the Good + Value of Life = Vision of Peace

The Mathematical and Philosophical Proof for World Peace

VG + VL = VP
VP = VG + VL
VP = V(G+L)
P = (G+L)
Peace = Good + Life
Peace = Good Life

PHOTON
SUPERHERO OF EDUCATION
www.BooksNotBombs.com

How to Ace a Math Test

The Highest Form of Pure Thought Is in Mathematics

PLATO
Ancient Greek Philosopher
428 BC-348 BC

How to Ace a Math Test

Math is learned by solving many types of problems. Math is cumulative. Every class builds on the previous one.

Tools of the Trade

Solving Math Problems
1. Think in steps: Step by step
2. Memorize the fundamentals
3. Translate abstract concepts into concrete terms

Ask Questions
Q1. What is given?
Q2. What is called for?
Q3. How many steps are required?
Q4. What operation must be used in each step?
Q5. Are the steps in the right order?
Q6. Check answer and make sure it is right

Math Errors
20% of All Math Errors Are Careless Mistakes
1. Write each number legibly.
2. Place two columns of figures exactly under one another.
3. Copy each problem correctly.

TOTAL RECALL: ACE EVERY TEST EVERY TIME

Steps to Success

In-Class Math Strategy: Take Organized Math Notes
Keep a list of the types of math problems solved and the sequence of steps:

Math Problem Type   Equations Used   Sequence of Steps

- As questions arise, ask your teacher for clarification.

- Don't leave class feeling lost, confused, and hopeless.

At-Home Math Strategy: Rework Class Problems
After every class, review your class notes and rework the math problems covered in class

Step 1. Write Out the Math Problem
- Read the word problem slowly and carefully.

- Remember this adage: Go slow to go fast.

- Slow is the way to accuracy and great grades.

- Write out the problem, number the steps, and double check what you've written.

- What are you trying to figure out? The last sentence of a word problem tells you what you are trying to find.

Step 2. Write Down the Information in the Problem

     Data   Variable   Equation

Word problems contain all the information needed to answer the question.

- List all the information given in the problem.

- Make two lists: Separate the knowns from the unknowns (the variable).

           Knowns   **Unknowns**

Q. What is the relationship between the known and the unknown values?

- Write an equation.

- Solve for the unknowns.

Step 3. What is the Best Math Method?
Make a plan and solve the problem. Develop a plan to solve the problem and solve it according to your plan.

Q1. How many steps does it take to solve the problem?

Q2. Does one part of the problem have to be solved before other parts can be solved?

Q3. Can the problem be divided into parts and solved separately?

Step 4. Check Your Work and Reread the Problem

- Check to see that you did not leave out any steps of your plan.

- Read problem again to see if your answer makes sense.

- Check answers for careless mistakes.

- Double check your calculator work immediately.

Step 5. Math Test Success Strategy

- Solve unassigned homework problems and see if you can finish them in the allotted time for the exam.

- Write big and bold. This will allow you to see a mistake and keep from confusing numbers, letters, or signs. Careless errors often creep in because you don't give yourself enough space to see and solve the problem.

- Answer the easy questions first to build your confidence. Budget your time.

- If you get stuck on a problem move on and come back to it later.

- Don't leave if you finish the exam early. Go back to the difficult problems.

- Use all of the available time to look for careless errors.

If You Think Dogs Can't Count,
Try Putting Three Dog Biscuits
in Your Pocket, and Then
Giving Fido Only Two of Them

Phil Pastoret

The Reward of a Thing Well
Done is to Have Done It

Ralph Waldo Emerson

Chapter 8
Good Grades Deserve Great Rewards

Put yourself in a state of mind where you say to yourself, here is an opportunity for you to celebrate like never before, my own power, my own ability to get myself to do whatever is necessary.

Anthony Robbins

Chapter 8

Good Grades Deserve Great Rewards

It only takes the first week of school to fall behind and start playing the game of catch-up. School will begin to feel like a non-stop roller coaster ride of books, papers, and tests. Once you complete a laborious academic assignment, stop and celebrate your success with a pleasurable reward of rest, recovery, and relaxation, known as "down time." Make a list of pleasurable rewards that you will receive once you have completed a mind-bending rigorous academic task.

Examples

Painstaking Academic Tasks	Pleasurable Rewards
Write Daily Test Review Notes	Music Concert
Ace English Essay	Movie
Ace Science Test	Dinner at Favorite Restaurant
Ace Research Report	Free Weekend of Play
Eat Healthy for Entire Week	Enjoy One Decadent Dessert
Maintain Regular Bedtime	Stay Out Late Saturday Night

COLLEGE LIFE

SUDOKO COLLEGE PUZZLES

Many college newspapers contains a daily Sudoko puzzle. College students find them entertaining and challenging.

What is a Sudoko puzzle?
It's a grid 9 squares wide and 9 squares deep.

4				2	8	3		
	8		1		4			2
7		6		8		5		
1				7		5		
2	7		5				1	9
	3		9	4				6
		8		9		7		5
3			8		6		9	
	4	2	7					3

The lines of squares running horizontally are called rows, and the lines running vertically are called columns.

The grid is further divided by the darker lines into nine 3 X 3 square 'boxes

The Rules
Some of the squares already have numbers in them.
Your task is to fill in the blank squares. There's only one rule: Each row, column and box must end up containing all of the numbers from 1 to 9. Each number can only appear once in a row, column or box.

SUDOKO PUZZLE STRATEGY
© By Paul Stephens

Here is Paul's strategy to solve a Sudoko puzzle:

1. Try slicing and dicing to solve any easy squares.

2. Crosshatch the entire puzzle box-by-box, pencilling-in complete candidate lists.

3. Scan the puzzle for the following rules:

Single-square candidates within an area (row/column/box) - solve immediately.

Claims by a box - remove the claimed candidate from the same row/column in other boxes.

Pairs within an area - remove the pair squares candidates from other lists within that area.

Triples within an area - remove the triple candidates from others lists within that area.

4. Whenever you solve a square, immediately check and update all candidate lists in the same row, column and box.

5. Whenever you've updated a candidate list, check to see if one of the rules now applies (e.g. you've created a triple, or a box is now claiming a number).

6. Never guess. Use logic. Have fun.

What If you could solve just one problem
in this world and by solving that one problem
you could solve every problem in the world?

If we just solve the "problem of education,"
then we could solve every problem in the
world: poverty, illiteracy, domestic violence,
religious strife, and war.

The human brain is the most powerful
biological machine in the world. What
would the world look like if educators
knew how to nurture and cultivate the
awesome power of the human brain?

When the seeds of peace are planted
within the minds and hearts of our children,
through education, then and only then,
will there be peace on earth. Our children
are our only hope for peace in the world,
and education is the only path to peace.

Sharon Rose Sugar
PALADIN OF EDUCATION

What All Parents Need to Know About Their Child's Education
THIS BOOK SAVES LIVES
"The Silent Crisis Destroying America's Brightest Minds"
"Book of the Month" Alma Public Library, Wisconsin

About Us

SMARTGRADES
BRAIN POWER REVOLUTION

Sharon Rose Sugar
The Paladin of Education for the 21st Century

Critical Contributions to Education

1. **SMARTGRADES BRAIN POWER REVOLUTION**
2. Education Paradigm: The Learning-Processing Education System
3. 40 Universal Gold Standards of Education
4. How to Nurture and Cultivate the Power of the Human Brain
5. How Does Learning Take Place
6. How to Measure Education

7. 8 Goalposts of Education:
    1. EDUCATION: KNOWLEDGE!
    2. ENLIGHTENMENT: AHA!
    3. EMPOWERMENT: YES I CAN!
    4. EXCELLENCE: MASTERY!
    5. EMANCIPATION: ALL CAN DO!
    6. EGALITARIANISM: EQUAL RIGHTS!
    7. EQUALITY: NEW WORLD ORDER!
    8. ECONOMIC STABILITY: WORLD PEACE!

8. Integration Therapy for Intrapersonal Growth, Development, and Maturity: 13 Steps to True and Everlasting Happiness

9. Feed the Whole Child: Mind, Body, and Spirit

10. Spiritual Affirmations: Empowerment, Responsibility, Special Gifts

11. The Silent Crisis Destroying America's Brightest Minds
    - The 15 Stumbling Blocks of Academic Failure
    - The 15 Stepping Stones to Academic Success
    - The Downward Spiral of Academic Failure
    - Academic Insanity
    - The Misdiagnosis of A.D.H.D., "The Incurable Brain Disorder"

12. The 3 Stages of Child Abuse: Cripple, Parasite, and Predator

13. Coined Word, "Democrisy," a Democracy Laden with Hypocrisy

14. PHOTON SUPERHERO OF EDUCATION, PhotonSuperhero.com

15. C.A.P.S. Children's Science Curriculum, Grades 1-4

16. In One Hour, Read Hebrew

Thinkers in Education

One Small Step for Women and One Giant Leap Forward for Education and World Peace.

Alain, Aristotle, Avicenna, Bello, Bettelheim, Binet, Blonsky, Al-Boustani, Buber, Cai Yuanpei, Claparede, Comenious, Condorcet, Confucius, Cousinet, Dawid, Decroly, Dewey, Diesterweg, Durkheim, Eotvos, Erasmus, Al-Farabi, Ferriere, Freinet, Freire, Freud, Frobel, Fukuzawa, Gandhi, Al-Ghazali, Giner de los Rios, Glinos, Goodman, Gramsci, Grundtvig, Grzegorzewska, Hegel, Herbart, Humbolt, Husen, Hussein, Illich, Jaspers, Jovellanos, Jullien de Paris, Kandel, Kant, Kerschensteiner, Key, Ibn Khaldun, Kold, Korczak, Krupskaya, Locke, Makarenko, Marti, Mencious, Miskawayh, Montaigne, Montessori, More, Naik, Neill, Noikov, Nyerere, Ortega y Gasset, Owen, Pestalozzi, Piaget, Plato, Priestley, Al-Qabbani, Read, Rogers, Rousseau, Rudenschold, Sadler, Salomon, Sarmiento, Sergio, Skinner, Spencer, Steiner, Suchodolski,
Sharon Rose Sugar (Sharon Esther Lampert)
PHOTON SUPERHERO OF EDUCATION,
Sun Yat-Sen, Tagore, Al-Tahtawi, Tolstoy, Trefort, Trstenjak, Ushinsky, Uznadze, Varela, Vasconcelos, Vico, Vives, Vygotsky, Wallon

My Super Heroine Pledge for World Peace

"I Pledge to Safeguard Your Mental Health,
Promote Mental Health in Your Family,
Create an Atmosphere of Peace Among Your Friends,
Inspire Good Will Among Your Neighbors, and Build a
Foundation of Stability in Your Community."

PHOTON
SUPERHERO OF EDUCATION
WWW.BOOKSNOTBOMBS.COM

WORLD PEACE IS COMING TO PLANET EARTH

The Official Emblem of

PHOTON

Super Hero Refresher Course

Clark Kent Is Superman

Bruce Wayne Is Batman

Peter Parker Is Spiderman

Diana Themyscira Is Wonder Woman

Sharon Rose Sugar Is Photon

SMART POWER IS BACK IN THE HANDS OF ALL STUDENTS

PHOTON'S
Spiritual Illuminations

5 SUPER POWERS TO MAKE YOUR DREAMS COME TRUE

1. TIME Is Nonrefundable
(Don't Waste Your Time)

2. ENERGY Is Rechargeable
(Set a Regular Bedtime)

3. MONEY Goes Round and Round
(You Have to Be in the Loop)

4. SELF-WORTH Is Infinite Potential
(Know Your Strengths, Iron Out Your weaknesses)

5. LOVE Everything You Touch
(Put Your Heart Into Everything)

WORLD PEACE IS COMING TO PLANET EARTH
www.BooksNotBombs.com

SMART POWER IS BACK IN THE HANDS OF ALL STUDENTS

PHOTON'S
Spiritual Illuminations

My Empowerment Affirmation

I have only one life.
My life is a valuable gift.
I am responsible for my destiny.
I changed my life to ensure my happiness.
Each day is lived fully with
purpose, enthusiasm, and joy.

WORLD PEACE IS COMING TO PLANET EARTH
www.BooksNotBombs.com

SEE THE WORLD THROUGH THE EYES OF A CREATIVE GENIUS

POETRY WORLD RECORD
120 WORDS OF RHYME FROM ONE FAMILY OF RHYME
Bible: "Through the Eyes of Eve"

THE WORLD TRADE CENTER TRAGEDY
"Spiraling Downward, Upward We Stand United"

Dr. Martin Luther King Jr.
"THE DELIVERER"

SIMON WIESENTHAL: NAZI HUNTER
"A Survivor's Burden"

Bible: CAIN & ABEL
"Cain & Abel: Inseparable-Together Forever"

"TSUNAMI" (Poet's Personal Favorite)

SUICIDE BOMBERS
"The Militant Palestinian Toddler Terrorist"

DARFUR
"There Is No Flower in Darfur"

THE IRAQ WAR
"Sandstorm in Baghdad"

KANSAS TWISTER
"The Return of Dorothy Gale"

KATRINA
"Drowning in the American Dream"

CENTRAL PARK VIOLENCE AGAINST WOMEN
"Water, Fight, Flight, and Tears"
(most published poem on the internet)

THE NEW YORK CITY BLACKOUT
"The Return of the Cavewoman"

Does Your Kid Read Sharon Esther Lampert?

Critical Contributions to Civilization

Prodigy
Unleash The Creator The God Within
10 Esoteric Laws of Genius & Creativity

The Awesome Art of Alliteration
Using One Letter of the Alphabet
Letters: C, D, E, P, S and T

Prophet
Who Knew God Was Such a Chatterbox

THE 22 COMMANDMENTS
All You Will Ever Need to Know About God

Philosopher Queen
- God of What? 11 Esoteric Laws of Inextricability
- The Sperm Manifesto: 10 Rules for the Road
- Women Have All The Power:
  But Have Never Learned How to Use It

Poet-22 Books of Poetry
- I Stole All The Words from The Dictionary

- **IMMORTALITY IS MINE**
  The Greatest Poems Ever Written on Extraordinary World Events

- **POETRY JEWELS**
  Diamonds, Emeralds, Sapphires, Rubies, and Pearls

- **V.E.S.S.E.L.**
  Very. Extra. Special. Sharon. Esther. Lampert.

How to Read a Poem By Sharon Esther Lampert

1. Similar to the poet William Blake, Sharon's poems are accompanied by elaborate visual graphics that enrich and compliment the text.

2. Sharon is a master of the art of condensation. She is able to condense a major world event in world history into a one page poem.

3. Sharon's poems are telescopic of the main event and microscopic of the infinite details.

4. Sharon's poems are known for her ability to weave poetry, philosophy, and comedy into a single verse.

5. Sharon's poems take you on a cinematic journey, and make you feel as if you are reliving the event, as if it happened today.

6. Many poets leave abandoned poems, that are unfinished. Sharon's poems are completed works of art. Every word is essential to the poem. You cannot remove or replace a word. There are no extra words. Every word has its rightful place and fits to perfection.

7. Sharon's poems are inspired. There are no rough drafts. Like giving birth to a baby, the poem incubates in her "creative apparatus" and is birthed in minutes. Like a baby, the poems are delivered whole and complete.

8. The last verse of every poem delivers a message that educates, enlightens, and empowers. Her searing signature endings seep under your skin, and find a way into your heart, and open your mind to a deeper understanding of the world.

Letter from Mommy, Age 9
Darling Sharon,
My Daughter is a Poet, Philosopher,
and Teacher.
Beauty & Brains.
Love and Kisses, XXX
Mommy (Eve Lampert)

SHARON ESTHER LAMPERT

The Sole Intention of My Poetry Is to Add Light to Your Soul.
Sharon Esther Lampert

See the World Through the Eyes of a Creative Genius

APRIL 30
NYC Poetry In Your Pocket Day

BE BORN

Be Born.
Become Educated.
Love Your Work.
Make a Meaningful Contribution -
To Yourself, Your Family, and Humanity.
Be a True Friend to Yourself First.
Have Sex with Someone You Love.
Make Love with Complete Abandon.
Enjoy Unconditional Love from Your Devoted Pet.
Make Time to Read the Funnies and Laugh.
Save Enough Money to Visit the Popular,
Pretty, and Peaceful Places of the World.
Read Great Literature, Listen to Great Music,
See Great Art, Watch the Great Movies,
Play the Fun Sports, Dance till Dawn,
Taste the Great Culinary Delights of the World -
Eat Slowly, Enjoy Every Bite, and Stay in Shape.
Plan One Great Adventure and Stick to the Plan.
Grow Old and Wise. Leave Your Money to
Someone You Love - Who Loves You Back.
Die in Your Sleep.

Sharon Esther Lampert

www.WorldFamousPoems.com
The Greatest Poems Ever Written on Extraordinary World Events

The Sole Intention of My Poetry Is to Add LIGHT to Your Soul

See the World Through the Eyes of a Creative Genius

THE 22 COMMANDMENTS
ALL YOU WILL EVER NEED TO KNOW ABOUT GOD
A UNIVERSAL MORAL COMPASS FOR ALL PEOPLE,
FOR ALL RELIGIONS, AND FOR ALL TIME

1. LIFE Over Death
2. STRENGTH Over Weakness
3. DEED Over Sin
4. LOVE Over Hatred
5. TRUTH Over Lie
6. WISDOM Over Stupidity
7. OPTIMISM Over Pessimism
8. SHARING Over Selfishness
9. PRAISE Over Criticism
10. LOYALTY Over Abandonment
11. RESPONSIBILITY Over Blame
12. GRATITUDE Over Envy
13. REWARD Over Punishment
14. ALLIES Over Enemies
15. CREATION Over Destruction
16. EDUCATION Over Ignorance
17. COOPERATION Over Competition
18. FREEDOM Over Oppression
19. COMPASSION Over Indifference
20. FORGIVENESS Over Revenge
21. PEACE Over War
22. JOY Over Suffering

Sharon Esther Lampert
Princess Kadimah: 8th Prophetess of Israel

www.PoetryJewels.com
Diamonds, Emeralds, Sapphires, Rubies, and Pearls

The Sole Intention of My Poetry Is to Add LIGHT to Your Soul

PHOTON
SUPERHERO of EDUCATION ®

EVERY DAY AN EASY A
3 Editions: Elementary, High School, College
ACE EVERY TEST EVERY TIME
All Global Bookstores

www.BooksNotBombs.com
EVERYBODY IS SOMEBODY SPECIAL

1 Minute Time Management Class
10 Steps to Success
EVERY DAY AN EASY A ©All Rights Reserved, 2010.

Step 1 ❑
Make a Daily Action Plan
Write Down Your Big Goals

Step 2 ❑
Set Your Priorities
Urgent, Important, Low, and Optional

Step 3 ❑
Breakdown Your Dreams
Breakdown Big Goal into Smaller Steps
List Steps Necessary to Complete Big Goal

Step 4 ❑
Divide and Conquer
Take Baby Steps Toward Reaching Goal
Crawl. Walk. Fly. Soar...

Step 5 ❑
Use Time Logs: Estimated Vs. Actual Time
e.g., Estimate Time for Lunch: 1 Hour
Actual Time: 20 Minutes
40 Minutes for Errands: Bank, Post Office, Store

Step 6 ❑
Life Is a Bumpy Road
Make Time for Delays, Detours,
Distractions, and Disappointments
e.g., Copier Runs Out of Toner and Paper

Step 7 ❑
Use Checkboxes to Keep Track of Completed Tasks

Step 8 ❑
Review and Refine Daily Action Plan
Pay Attention to Strengths and Weaknesses

Step 9 ❑
Celebrate Your Success
Celebrate Job Well Done with Daily Reward

Step 10 ❑
EVERY DAY AN EASY A
www.everydayaneasya.com

www.ingramcontent.com/pod-product-compliance
Lightning Source LLC
Chambersburg PA
CBHW070538170426
43200CB00011B/2467